EMPATH CHILDREN

How to Help a Highly Sensitive Child Thrive and Stop Feeling Overwhelmed

BY JUDY DYER

EMPATH CHILDREN: How to Help a Highly Sensitive Child
Thrive and Stop Feeling Overwhelmed
by Judy Dyer

© **Copyright 2021 by Judy Dyer**

All Rights Reserved.

Disclaimer: This book is designed to provide accurate and authoritative information in regard to the subject matter covered. By its sale, neither the publisher nor the author is engaged in rendering psychological or other professional services. If expert assistance or counseling is needed, the services of a competent professional should be sought.

ISBN: 979-8736526505

ALSO BY JUDY DYER

Empath: A Complete Guide for Developing Your Gift and Finding Your Sense of Self

The Empowered Empath: A Simple Guide on Setting Boundaries, Controlling Your Emotions, and Making Life Easier

The Highly Sensitive: How to Stop Emotional Overload, Relieve Anxiety, and Eliminate Negative Energy

Empath and The Highly Sensitive: 2 in 1 Bundle

Empaths and Narcissists: 2 in 1 Bundle

CONTENTS

INTRODUCTION

Most adults are tuned in to their emotions; when they are happy, sad, angry or frustrated, they know why. But children are too young to understand the range of human emotions we experience, and these feelings can be overwhelming for them. For empath children, it is significantly worse. Not only are they forced to deal with the complexities of their own feelings, but they also carry everyone else's emotions around with them. Empaths are also referred to as 'highly sensitive.' Throughout this book, these terms will be used interchangeably.

High sensitivity is not a psychological disorder, it is a personality trait. If you are responsible for a highly sensitive child (HSC), it is essential that you have a full understanding of the complexities of this gift or you will unintentionally damage your child. Children are emotional creatures, but it can be difficult to assess the emotions of empath children because of their innate nature. However, establishing an emotional connection with them is essential because they need to know they are understood and valued.

Children need adults in their lives who believe in them, and who will encourage them to live out their purpose, regardless of the labels ascribed to them. They may be strong in many areas, but empath children are also exceptionally vulnerable, and can become overwhelmed, anxious, numb or exhausted, often without any warning.

The only way to build an emotional connection with a highly sensitive child is to communicate that you care, want to support them and help them become all they were destined to be without compromising their authentic selves.

I wrote this book because I was an empath child that nobody (not even my parents or siblings) understood. I was bullied at home and at school, and was often banished to my room or punished in some other way for my reactions to things that I had no control over. I was told I was too emotional, over the top, too sensitive and any other negative adjective associated with being a highly sensitive person. As a result, I became extremely insecure. I was a social recluse for many years and rarely socialized with friends and family. I remember being a loud and boisterous child, but my personality was literally bullied out of me and I became shy, timid and introverted.

It wasn't until I was in my early twenties studying psychology at college and one of my modules was on empaths that I started looking into it. I began reading and researching empaths and learned that there was nothing wrong with me after all. It was a very liberating time; I could now understand the feelings and challenges I was constantly dealing with.

My childhood and teenage years were the worst because my parents, siblings and teachers lacked any knowledge about empath children. Now I have the opportunity to give someone a head start and provide all the answers I wish someone could have given to *my* parents when I was a child.

Those who understand high sensitivity must take a stand against a society that refuses to celebrate diversity and has a negative tendency to label people according to their own norms and values. Highly sensitive children are unique and extraordinary individuals who have an abundance of talents to offer the world, and they must be celebrated as such.

Let us use our voices to give empath children a firm and secure space in the world and stop limiting and labelling the possibilities of who they have the potential to be. Whether you are a parent, caregiver, teacher or role model, we all have the power to make a difference. With every word of encouragement, every time we protect and defend our children, we are building a strong community of empaths.

In this book you will find practical strategies to help your empath children thrive when things overwhelm them. In turn, they will grow into assertive, confident adults who are fully equipped to navigate this rough and tumble world as empath people.

In order to maximize the value you receive from this book, I strongly encourage you to join our tight-knit community on Facebook. Here you will be able to connect and share with other like-minded empaths and parents to continue your growth.

Taking this journey alone is not recommended, and this can be an excellent support network for you.

It would be great to connect with you there,

Judy Dyer

To Join, Visit:
www.pristinepublish.com/empathgroup

Or Scan the QR Code on Your Phone:

DOWNLOAD THE AUDIO VERSION OF THIS BOOK FREE

If you love listening to audiobooks on the go or would enjoy a narration as you read along, I have great news for you. You can download the audio book version of *Empath Children* for FREE (Regularly $14.95) just by signing up for a FREE 30-day audible trial!

Visit: www.pristinepublish.com/audiobooks

Or Scan the QR Code on Your Phone:

YOUR FREE GIFT -
HEYOKA EMPATH

A lot of empaths feel trapped, as if they've hit a glass ceiling they can't penetrate. They know there's another level to their gift, but they can't seem to figure out what it is. They've read dozens of books, been to counselling, and confided in other experienced empaths, but that glass ceiling remains. They feel alone, and alienated from the rest of the world because they know they've got so much more to give, but can't access it. Does this sound like you?

The inability to connect to your true and authentic self is a tragedy. Being robbed of the joy of embracing the full extent of your humanity is a terrible misfortune. The driving force of human nature is to live according to one's own sense of self, values, and emotions. Since the beginning of time, philosophers, writers, and scholars have argued that authenticity is one of the most important elements of an individual's well-being.

When there's a disconnect between a person's inner being and their expressions, it can be psychologically damaging. Heyokas are the most powerful type of empaths, and many of them are not fully aware of who they are. While other empaths experience feelings of overwhelm and exhaustion from absorbing others' energy and emotions, heyoka empaths experience an additional aspect of exhaustion in that they are fighting a constant battle with their inability to be completely authentic.

The good news is that the only thing stopping you from becoming your authentic self is a lack of knowledge. You need to know exactly who you are so you can tap into the resources that have been lying dormant within you. In this bonus e-book, you'll gain in-depth information about the seven signs that you're a heyoka empath, and why certain related abilities are such powerful traits. You'll find many of the answers to the questions you've been searching for your entire life such as:

- Why you feel uncomfortable when you're around certain people
- How you always seem to find yourself on the right path even though your decisions are not based on logic or rationale
- The reason you get so offended when you find out others have lied to you
- Why you analyze everything in such detail
- The reason why humor is such an important part of your life
- Why you refuse to follow the crowd, regardless of the consequences
- The reason why strangers and animals are drawn to you

There are three main components to authenticity: understanding who you are, expressing who you are, and letting the world experience who you are. Your first step on this journey is to know who you are, and with these seven signs that you're a heyoka empath, you'll find out. I've included snippets about the first three signs in this description to give you full confidence that you're on the right track:

Sign 1: You Feel and Understand Energy

Heyoka empaths possess a natural ability to tap into energy. They can walk into a room and immediately discern the atmosphere.

When an individual walks past them, they can literally see into their soul because they can sense the aura that person is carrying. But empaths also understand their own energy, and they allow it to guide them. You will often hear this ability referred to as "the sixth sense." The general consensus is that only a few people have this gift. But the reality is that everyone was born with the ability to feel energy; it's just been demonized and turned into something spooky, when in actual fact, it's the most natural state to operate in.

Sign 2: You are Led by Your Intuition

Do you find that you just know things? You don't spend hours, days, and weeks agonizing over decisions, you can just feel that something is the right thing to do, and you go ahead and do it. That's because you're led by your intuition and you're connected to the deepest part of yourself. You know your soul, you listen to it, and you trust it. People like Oprah Winfrey, Steve Jobs and Richard Branson followed their intuition steadfastly and it led them to become some of the most successful people in the history of the world. Living from within is the way we were created to be, and those who trust this ability will find their footing in life a lot more quickly than others. Think of it as a GPS system: when it's been programmed properly, it will always take you to your destination via the fastest route.

Sign 3: You Believe in Complete Honesty

In general, empaths don't like being around negative energy, and there's nothing that can shift a positive frequency faster than dishonesty. Anything that isn't the truth is a lie, even the tiny ones that we excuse away as "white lies." And as soon as they're released from someone's mouth, so is negative energy. Living an authentic life requires complete honesty at all times, and although the truth may hurt, it's better than not being able to trust someone. Heyoka empaths get very uncomfortable in the presence of liars. They are fully aware that the vibrations of the person don't match the words they are saying. Have you ever experienced a brain freeze mid-conversation? All of a sudden you just couldn't think straight, you couldn't articulate yourself properly, and things just got really awkward? That's because your empath antenna picked up on a lie.

Heyoka Empath: 7 Signs You're A Heyoka Empath & Why It's So Powerful is a revolutionary tool that will help you transition from uncertainty to complete confidence in who you are. In this easy-to-read guide, I will walk you through exactly what makes you a heyoka empath. I've done the research for you, so no more spending hours, days, weeks, and even years searching for answers, because everything you need is right here in this book.

You have a deep need to share yourself with the world, but you've been too afraid because you knew something was missing. The information within the pages of this book is the missing piece in the jigsaw puzzle of your life. There's no turning back now!

Get *Heyoka Empath* for Free by Visiting

www.pristinepublish.com/empathbonus

Or Scan the QR Code on Your Phone:

CHAPTER 1:

THE CHARACTERISTICS OF AN EMPATH CHILD

Empaths feel other people's energy, emotions and physical symptoms as if they were their own. Dr. Judith Orloff, one of the forerunners in the field, refers to empaths as 'emotional sponges' who absorb everything around them whether it's good or bad. Orloff is the author of *The Empath's Survival Guide: Life Strategies for Sensitive People*. In it, she states that empaths do not have the ability to protect themselves against excessive stimulation. Therapist Kim Egel suggests that empaths are highly sensitive to outside stimuli, such as chaotic environments, boisterous people and loud noise. They feel things on a very deep level; they are exceptionally caring and bring light into dark places.

The term 'empath' has its roots in the word 'empathy.' Empathy is the ability to understand things from the perspective of the person who is going through it. For example, if your spouse is upset because they have lost their job, empathy gives you the ability to connect with their pain despite the fact that you have never lost your job before. But empaths add another dimension to this: they can actually feel and sense the emotions their spouse is experiencing because they have been replicated in the empath person. In other words, if a person is happy, so are they; if someone is sad, so are they.

Being an empath child is incredibly challenging; empaths find it difficult to remain in the same space as other people because it causes overwhelm and they lose themselves. As a result, empath children often suffer from extreme loneliness. Even though they want to connect, it causes them too much turmoil and they are forced to pull away. Empath children can also experience a 'frayed nerve' feeling, or sensory overload due to too much touching or talking. But because children don't know how to express such feelings, it often results in outbursts or meltdowns. Parents who don't understand the nature of an empath can get very frustrated with this constant rollercoaster of emotions.

You might suspect your child is an empath, but you are not sure. Here are some of the most common characteristics in empath children:

- Experiences deep feelings
- Does better when strangers are not present
- Won't climb onto something unless they've checked it for safety
- Notices things that would normally go unnoticed
- Doesn't like noisy environments
- Doesn't tolerate pain
- Asks a lot of meaningful questions
- Enjoys playing quietly
- A perfectionist
- Always asking questions
- Wants to change out of dirty clothes immediately
- Has psychic abilities
- Doesn't like change

- Finds it difficult to sleep
- Very intuitive
- Picks up on smells
- Appears to read your mind
- Responds better to gentle correction than harsh discipline
- Hates being surprised
- Can't wear scratchy clothing like labels in socks
- Easily startled

THE ADVANTAGES OF BEING AN EMPATH CHILD

Despite the many challenges that empaths face due to the nature of this personality trait, there are also many advantages associated with being an empath, here are some of them:

- **They Are Creative:** Because of their heightened sensitivity, empaths can connect with their inner being in a way the average person can't. This ability accelerates creativity which is why they are often extremely gifted.

- **They Have a Ceaseless Imagination:** They are dreamers and very inventive. HSCs can get lost in their own imagination and find it difficult to return to reality. They are well known for intense daydreaming.

- **They Are Fair:** Empath children know the difference between right and wrong because they can feel people's pain. When an injustice is taking place, you can guarantee an empath child will stand-up in the victim's defense.

- **They Make Great Friends:** They are extremely loyal, very generous, genuine and respectful. Because they care so much about other people's feelings, they do everything possible to ensure they never hurt anyone.

- **They Are Passionate:** When an HSC finds something they love, they put their heart and soul into it in a way that the average person will not. They become totally dedicated and committed to it.

- **They Are Compassionate:** Because they are so in tune with other people's feelings, they can sense what others are going through. The highly sensitive child will do everything they can to make someone feel better.

- **They Appreciate Nature:** Empaths connect with nature on a very deep level; they enjoy doing things like walking in the grass with their bare feet because it restores them. Highly sensitive children can sense the gifts that the earth carries, and they are inspired by them.

- **They Are Original:** Empaths don't think like the average person. They evaluate things on a much deeper level and provide insight into things that others can't see.

- **They Can't be Deceived:** Because they are so in touch with their surroundings, they can sense when something isn't quite right. Highly sensitive children always know when someone is lying.

- **They Are Intensely Happy:** Because HSCs are deeply connected to their emotions, when they are happy, they are exceptionally happy because they can feel it more intensely.

WHY EMPATH CHILDREN BECOME A PROBLEM

Not much is understood about the HSC, and as a result, they are often misjudged or labeled as having some type of behavioral disorder because they don't act and react like 'normal' children. Now, I am not going to get into a debate about 'normal' and 'abnormal' children. As far as I am concerned, empath children are normal, but the reality is they are different. Nevertheless, the benefits only become visible when that difference is understood.

Humans understand their world by processing the information they are presented with. To do this successfully, we need time to think about, reflect on and process the things that are taking place. How we do this depends on the person; some like to talk, others to sing, dance, write, draw or go somewhere that's quiet and reflect. When a teacher doesn't understand highly sensitive children and he/she is resolving a situation in the classroom, when the child doesn't react in a way that conforms to the norms and standards of their expectations, discipline is administered even when the child wasn't being disobedient, they were reacting in the only way they know how.

For example, a child might need to sing or dance to express themselves, but in class they are only allowed to work quietly, and their normal way of expressing themselves is seen as a distraction. This causes the child to become overwhelmed which can cause a meltdown. However, this reaction is more common in creative empath children.

THE IMPORTANCE OF A DIAGNOSIS

Self-diagnosis for your highly sensitive child is a step forward, but a professional diagnosis is better. Not only do you want to be certain about it, you also want to reap all the benefits that come with it.

To start, don't allow the word 'diagnosis' to scare you. There is nothing wrong with your child, he/she is not ill and nor do they suffer from a mental disorder.

The Path to a Diagnosis: Unless you are an empath yourself, you won't know your child is an empath, and you will most likely face a difficult journey to discover this truth. It often starts with a passing comment – a teacher, a parent or medical professional might pick it up and question you about it. People who are familiar with the highly sensitive trait will notice things like how upset your child gets when someone else is in distress. Or a schoolteacher will notice the fear they experience when separated from their parents. It is not uncommon for parents of empath children to become extremely frustrated, and when they find out their child is not just acting up they are quick to start an investigation.

It is also important to mention that medical professionals won't use the term 'empath' to diagnose your child because the characteristic is most commonly referred to as 'highly sensitive.' A highly sensitive diagnosis isnot the same as a diagnosis for a condition such as ADHD or autism. High sensitivity has not been recorded in a diagnostic manual, and according to psychologist Elaine Aron, this is because when a trait is found in 15 to 20% of the population, it is considered normal. But at the same time, it is not prevalent enough to be understood by most people.

A professional will often go down the road of ruling out everything else on their checklist before acknowledging that a child is highly sensitive. They will put the label on a report, but because high sensitivity doesn't require medication, counseling or therapy, it is not considered an 'official' diagnosis.

A Label Makes Your Life Easier: The institution you are going to have most problems with when it comes to your highly sensitive child is the school system. Unless your child's school has a full understanding of high sensitivity, they are most likely going to give you a cold blank stare when you approach them. As you will read in

Chapter 11, highly sensitive children are often labeled in the wrong way by their teachers who have no understanding of this personality trait. However, when you go to the school with a report from a professional, it will increase your chances of getting the support you need.

CHAPTER 2:

THE IMPORTANCE OF EARLY CHILDHOOD BONDING

S trong relationships are essential for children, and even more so for empath children. Life is full of challenges, and not one of us is exempt from adversity, so your early childhood years will determine how you recover from those negative events. Resilience is an essential character trait for overcoming trials, and it is essential that the highly sensitive child develops it so they can thrive in a world that has limited understanding of their personality type.

FORMING ATTACHMENTS DURING THE FIRST YEARS OF LIFE

Babies are born with a natural desire to attach to their parents. They need love and attention, and they are completely dependent on the people who brought them into the world. Unfortunately, some parents/caregivers have no desire to bond with their children, but this doesn't undo the natural desire babies have for bonding. This attachment is the foundation upon which the child's sense of self develops. Everything, from their self-esteem to values about self and confidence, are the result of this first attachment.

The reality is that many children develop feelings of low self-worth and low self-esteem during childhood. There are several reasons for this, but one of them is that we live in a world where societal expectations sometimes force people into situations they are not ready for. There is still a stigma attached to women who are not married with children by the age of 30 or 35. As a result, children are born out of dysfunctional relationships and the negative cycle begins. People who are not ready to be parents are not going to have the skills required to raise emotionally stable children. If you recognize that you fall into this category, your first step should be to seek counseling so you can effectively raise your child, because highly sensitive children require more time, attention, and energy than the average child.

Consistency is key with infants because they need the same level of love, care and nurturing at all times, and they need unconditional love. There may be days when you don't feel like being overly affectionate with your child because of their bad behavior. But withholding love in the form of words of affirmation, hugs and kisses is one of the worst things you can do to an empath child. It reinforces the notion that they are only worthy of love when people are happy with their behavior. This leads to the dangerous cycle of suppressing feelings, and for an HSC, not being able to express their feelings can be detrimental to their overall mental well-being.

Research suggests that the first five years of a child's life are the most important, as that is when the brain develops and character traits and patterns of behavior are established. Babies grow into emotionally stable children when their caregivers are able to tune into their needs. The way a child views the world will depend on these early interactions, and if they are bad, they will develop a negative perception of life.

A parent with high emotional intelligence who understand their own needs, will be capable of effectively tuning into their child's needs. When an infant is cared for in this way, they experience security, stability and a deep emotional connection with the caregiver. Most importantly, when this level of care is administered consistently, it hardwires the pre-frontal cortex, which is the part of the brain responsible for thinking. As a result, resilience or the ability to self-regulate and reflect, is developed. Children learn empathy from their parents. In general, an empathetic adult was raised by empathetic parents.

This bond starts in the womb, where the child has a secure foundation upon which to build, and it is from this lens that he/she views the world. A newborn baby can only communicate their needs by crying. They will scream, holler and writhe until they get the attention of their mother. When she provides comfort and soothing, the baby experiences relief from their troubles and the mother also experiences relief knowing that the child is well. The same takes place with the father, and each time the baby's needs are met, neural pathways are formed in the brain that lead them to subconsciously expect loving, kind and genuine relationships from the people they meet.

A baby crying causes an increase in neural activity in both the baby's and the mother's brains. This is a part of the connection process. Italian neurophysiologist Giacomo Rizzolatti coined this response, 'mirror neurons' in the early 1990s. His research has given us deeper insight into how humans empathize with each other and offer appropriate responses. You will notice that when there are two babies in a room, when one starts crying, in most cases, the other will start crying too. When a parent is feeding their child, they will open their mouth at the same time. Even people who are not parents can testify to feeling someone else's pain when they see them get injured.

A positive response when a child's needs are met is the way children develop the skill of self-regulation; they then carry it into adulthood. If an infant receives consistent soothing when they are in distress, it forms the biological framework required for dealing with stress in the future. This action is known as co-regulation, and it helps the child develop their own sense of internal security as they learn to self-soothe and calm themselves down during times of stress. When a parent does not act consistently with calming and soothing behavior, as the child grows, they will find it difficult to self-regulate their emotions, and that condition will manifest through their behavior.

CHILDREN AND THEIR NEED FOR AN EMOTIONAL CONNECTION

Children feel safe when they have a secure bond with their parents. It is where they go for comfort and safety, and it is how children learn to regulate their emotions. During these times of comfort, the child also learns how to express their feelings. For example, after a fall, the parent might say something like, *"Hurting yourself like that can make you feel scared can't it? I want to know if you feel upset, scared or sad at the moment."* With each encounter, the child develops the skill of reflective thinking, and they become familiar with different words to articulate their emotions. It is essential that children learn to put their feelings into words from an early age, because that is how people overcome trauma and stress.

When children do not experience this articulation of emotions in their early years, they will feel very uncomfortable when asked to express their feelings. Managing strong emotions is not something they are familiar with, and instead of expressing themselves verbally, they will act out. They then find it difficult to develop meaningful relationships because they tend to either lash out or walk away when strong feelings emerge. This behavior leads to a vicious cycle of fear and the inability to trust. When children are raised in an environment where this pattern of behavior is present, they will carry it into adulthood unless there is an intervention from someone who has a positive impact on the child's life by spending enough time in their company to teach them these skills.

When children are not given the space to express their feelings without it being met with a negative response, they will resort to coping mechanisms that those around them will find difficult to deal with. Resilience is developed through stress; when feelings of fear and anxiety arise, the presence of a secure, reassuring, comforting adult provides relief from those feelings. However, when they do not get the relief they need, the skill set they need to recover when they get older is never learned.

TWO KEY CHARACTERISTICS FOR HEALTHY DEVELOPMENT

Kindness and empathy lay the foundation for a child to develop and grow into an emotionally healthy adult. However, it is extremely difficult to maintain consistency with this mental caregiving because children are really good at getting on your nerves. They tend to push boundaries and will do whatever it takes to get a reaction out of you. Children are like sponges; they absorb everything that takes place in their environment. So on the days when you just can't take it anymore and you snap, they're learning exactly how they will react when they feel they can't take it anymore. On the other hand, when their bad behavior is met with empathy, kindness and patience, they too will develop these qualities. This is not to say that you should allow your children to walk all over you. It is possible to exhibit these traits while at the same time being firm. However, it is more than understandable that there are times when you and your child will fly off the handle and say things you regret. The key is to ensure that it becomes the norm to apologize to each other immediately after things get heated. Not only will this further solidify the bond between you and your child, it will also provide a healthy example of how they are to behave when they start forming relationships.

THE FREEDOM OF SELF-EXPRESSION

It is natural for parents to have dreams and goals for their children. A parent with a successful career as a doctor will often want their child to become a doctor or other professional. A father will often want his sons to get involved in sports because he believes it is the ultimate expression of masculinity. However, if he/she doesn't express an interest in these things it can lead to what is referred to as mis-attunement. That involves the child feeling that they are not accepted by their parents. This is often the case with highly sensitive boys, as they are typically creatives and have no interest in physically competitive activities. As a result, the child feels rejected by their father, and that can have a detrimental effect on his/her emotional development. Highly sensitive children need to feel understood because when they don't, it is traumatizing and confusing for them, which results in them isolating themselves.

As you are probably aware, sensitive children often find it difficult to deal with events that the average child would brush off as a part of life. When parents react with anger instead of trying to view life through the same lens as their child, that can have a negative effect on their relationship. When HSCs cry over things like a person who looks upset, music playing, or an animal getting injured in a film, they look to you as the caregiver to help them understand their feelings. When emotions are met with scorn, the child will start feeling shame and embarrassment about their feelings.

THE MISTAKES PARENTS MAKE RAISING EMPATH CHILDREN

This section is in no way meant to bash parents of empath children who make mistakes, because there is no such thing as having it all together. You can implement every strategy mentioned in this book and still not get it right. There is no such thing as the perfect parent and there never will be. Parents of highly sensitive children seem to be harder on themselves than others because it feels like no matter what they do, they can't get anything right. However, you can make life a lot easier for yourself if you know what mistakes to avoid, so here are some of the most common ones.

Putting Labels on HSCs: 'Shy, wild, timid sissy' are some of the labels often ascribed to HSCs. Highly sensitive children express themselves in a variety of ways, and unless these behaviors are understood, they are often mislabeled. You often find that once these labels have been applied, they stick, and they become a self-fulfilling prophecy. Instead of a child embracing the fact that they are highly sensitive, they become the label.

Thinking Hypersensitivity Must be Corrected: This is especially true for boys; often times, parents fear their highly sensitive boys will become homosexual because they are seen as too emotional. Additionally, parents fear their highly sensitive girls will grow up to be selfish and hysterical because it appears their emotions are out of control.

Parents typically respond to 'overly emotional' children by forcing them not to express their emotions. This is the worst thing a parent can do because it puts too much pressure and tension on the child's nervous system, and eventually, this will manifest as tantrums, disruptions and in more severe cases later on, depression.

Over-Protection: When a parent doesn't understand the characteristics of highly sensitive children, they become overprotective. However, an increasing number of studies prove that overprotective parenting has a negative effect on children. Overprotective parenting involves the following:

- Excessive caution
- Micromanagement and constant supervision
- Controlling their child's social environment
- Comforting their children too quickly
- Strict rules
- Overemphasis on reward and punishment
- Harsh discipline

Because of the characteristics of empath children, it is not uncommon for their parents to want to shelter them. If each time they come home from school, a friend or a relative's house, they are upset, overwhelmed or have a meltdown, it's only normal for a parent to want to shield their child from such experiences. But despite the parent's good intentions, that sheltering impacts the child's behavior later in life. Research suggests that overprotected children grow up to be co-dependent, immature, and entitled.

CHAPTER 3:

ANXIETY DISORDERS IN EMPATH CHILDREN

Empath children are prone to anxiety disorders; it's important that you know as much about the condition as possible so you are better equipped to deal with it when it shows up. The good news is that not all sensitive children will suffer from a full-blown anxiety disorder. They may go through mild periods of the condition where it's not necessary for them to seek medical assistance, but you can coach them through it instead.

WHAT IS AN ANXIETY DISORDER?

Anxiety disorders are characterized by irrational and persistent fear and overwhelming worry that interrupts normal life. They affect the normal functioning of the brain and they also manifest as physical symptoms such as stomach aches, headaches, jitteriness, sleeplessness and irritability.

The condition prevents children from speaking up in class, making friends or taking part in social or school activities. Children can also experience feelings of shame and fear. Research suggests that if an anxiety disorder is left to fester, it can cause other conditions such as attention deficit hyperactivity disorder (ADHD), eating disorders and depression.

ANXIETY DISORDER OR NOT?

All children will experience anxiety at some stage during their childhood. They may go through phases where they only eat yellow foods, or they've got to do everything twice. Others may experience speaking to invisible 'friends' or they may have constant nightmares that there is a boogie man in the closet.

Some children will experience anxiety as a temporary phase, meaning they will shift in and out of it every so often, and it's generally harmless. Conversely, a child suffering from an anxiety disorder will go through continuous feelings of shyness, nervousness and fear; they may refuse to go to certain places or engage with others; and no matter how hard parents, teachers or caregivers try to smooth the way, these feelings persist.

A temporary phase is typically triggered by something your child might have watched on TV, which makes it difficult for them to fall asleep. Parents and caregivers can usually soothe children out of these temporary feelings of fear. But when it's an anxiety disorder, the child is unable to get past their fear.

Anxiety disorders deteriorate the psyche over time, and you will witness a noticeable difference in your child's behavior. To be on the safe side, it is advised that you take your child to the doctor, who will refer you to a mental health specialist and run the appropriate tests to determine whether it's an anxiety disorder or not.

ANXIETY DISORDERS - WHAT ARE THE CAUSES?

Besides the fact that your child is highly sensitive, there are other factors that contribute to anxiety disorders in children. According to experts, they are caused by a range of environmental and biological factors similar to diabetes and allergies. Events such as the death of a grandparent or parent, changing schools, and parents getting divorced can act as triggers.

It is also normal for anxiety disorders to run in families, but they are not always passed down to children. It is also important to mention that if your child is diagnosed with an anxiety disorder, it is not an indication of bad parenting, nor is it a sign of weakness.

TYPES OF ANXIETY DISORDERS

There are several types of anxiety disorders and it will benefit you to know about the most common ones, which are as follows:

GENERALIZED ANXIETY DISORDER (GAD)

This type of anxiety causes your child to worry excessively about different things including:

- Punctuality
- Performance in sports
- Grades
- Health
- Natural disasters
- Relationships with peers

General anxiety disorder also causes physical symptoms such as:

- Irritability
- Inability to focus
- Restlessness
- Fatigue
- Difficulty falling asleep

Children with GAD spend a lot of time scrutinizing themselves, they long for perfection and are constantly looking for approval from others.

PANIC DISORDER

When a child has more than one panic attack for no reason, it is likely that a mental health professional will diagnose them with a panic disorder. Experiencing at least four of the following symptoms is a sign that your child is having a panic attack:

- Hot flushes or chills
- Tingling sensations
- A fear of dying
- A fear of going insane
- A sense of depersonalization
- Light-headedness or dizziness
- Abdominal discomfort or dizziness
- Chest pain
- A choking feeling
- A feeling of being smothered or shortness of breath
- Trembling
- Sweating
- Rapid heartbeat
- The need to escape
- The feeling that something bad is about to happen

It is not uncommon for children to develop agoraphobia (a fear of places and situations' when the panic attack occurred). It is normal for children who have had panic attacks at school to refuse to go back.

POST-TRAUMATIC STRESS DISORDER (PTSD)

After witnessing or experiencing a life-threatening event, children become prone to post traumatic stress disorder. Such events might include a natural disaster, physical abuse, violent assault or a car accident. The condition involves experiencing extreme anxiety and fear, constant irritability or the inability to connect with their emotions.

The traumatic events will often revisit the child through flashbacks or nightmares, or they will re-create them during playtime. PTSD can make it difficult for children to sleep and to concentrate when they are in school or trying to do homework. Other symptoms include isolating themselves from friends and family, getting startled by loud noises, and unjustified nervousness about their surroundings. It is not uncommon for children to experience symptoms many months or years after the event.

Not all children who witness or experience a traumatic event will suffer from PTSD. Fear and anxiety is a normal reaction when something frightening happens to a child, but for most children, these feelings are only temporary. Those who are most prone to developing PTSD are generally children who already suffer from a mental illness or were directly affected by the incident through injury or the death of a parent. Children with limited support, or those who witness violence in the home are also at increased risk of suffering from PTSD after a traumatic event.

SEPARATION ANXIETY DISORDER

Separation anxiety disorder generally affects children between the ages of 18 months and 3 years. It is normal for children in this age group to experience anxiety when they can't see their parents or when parents leave the room. Toddlers will cry excessively when they start day-care or preschool, but it is possible to distract children from these feelings, and this usually happens once they start engaging with their new environment and find activities to occupy their mind.

When older children react to their parents leaving them with a relative or a babysitter, and it is difficult to calm them down, there is a possibility they are suffering from separation anxiety disorder. Children between the ages of seven and nine are most likely to suffer from this condition.

Symptoms of separation anxiety include feelings of misery or extreme homesickness, demanding that they sleep in their parents' bed at night, refusal to go to school or a sleepover because they are afraid of being away from loved ones. Children with separation anxiety fear that something bad will happen to them or their caregivers while they are apart.

SELECTIVE MUTISM

Some children will refuse to speak in situations where it is necessary or expected. Their unwillingness to communicate makes it difficult for them to make friends or participate in school and social activities. There are several reasons why children develop selective mutism, but it is generally believed to be a form of severe social anxiety. However, since there are many other factors that could be at play, it is typically not diagnosed as an anxiety disorder.

SYMPTOMS OF SELECTIVE MUTISM

There are several symptoms associated with this condition; instead of talking, children will do the following:

- Avoid eye contact
- Retreat into a corner
- Twirl the hair

- Chew on the hair
- Turn their head
- Stand expressionless
- Stand motionless

The reason why the condition is referred to as 'selective' mutism is because children are normally very talkative when they are in comfortable surroundings. Parents find it hard to believe when a teacher or a caregiver informs them that their child refused to speak, because they know them as talkative and outgoing with not a shy bone in their body. Children are usually diagnosed when they start school or between the ages of four and eight.

SOCIAL ANXIETY DISORDER

Social anxiety disorder is also referred to as 'social phobia'; it manifests as an extreme fear of social activities and performances. It can have a negative effect on a child's school attendance and performance, while they also find it difficult to make and keep friends. There are many other symptoms of social anxiety disorder including:

- Discomfort, passivity and hesitance in the spotlight
- Inability to speak when asked a question or to read aloud in class
- Excessive concern about embarrassment, humiliation or negative evaluation
- Sitting alone in the cafeteria or library, or refusing to go to team meetings or to socialize in groups
- Mumbling or speaking in a low tone
- Avoiding eye contact with peers or adults
- Refusing to start conversations, send an email, call or text their friends, refusal to order food at restaurants

SPECIFIC PHOBIAS

A specific phobia is one in which children experience extreme feelings of fear about a situation such as swimming or an object like a cat. It is normal for children to have fears and they eventually grow out of them. However, if the fear lasts longer than six months and hinders them from engaging in normal activities, such as going to school so they don't have to participate in the thing they are afraid of, they may have a specific phobia. Children usually have phobias of medical procedures, the dark, blood, water, heights, storms and animals.

Children typically respond to phobias through complete avoidance, or when they face their fears, they will have a physical reaction such as stomach aches, headaches, clinging to parents, tantrums and crying. Children do not have the mental capacity to understand that their fear is irrational; therefore, they become completely invested in the fear because they believe it's justified.

HOW IS ANXIETY DISORDER TREATED?

Once a diagnosis has been established, healthcare professionals will determine the best treatment option available for your child. According to research, there are several treatments that work well for children, the most common being a combination of medication and cognitive behavioral therapy (CBT).

All children are different, therefore, what works for one might not work for another. Or one child might respond to the treatment immediately, and it might take longer for another child. Having a discussion with your doctor will assist in making the right choices for your child over the long term. It is also important to mention that your child may have a different response to the treatment over time. In general, these are the treatment options you can expect:

MEDICATION

A psychologist may advise that your child take prescription medication to treat their anxiety disorder. It is not uncommon to combine medication with therapy. One study found that when anti-depressants are administered at the same time as undergoing cognitive behavioral therapy, it works better than a single treatment alone for children between the ages of 7 and 17.

Medication is either a short- or long-term solution, depending on the severity of your child's condition, and how they respond to treatment. Your doctor will be able to give additional advice about this. You will also need to inform your doctor if your child is taking any other medication, to prevent them from having an adverse reaction to the prescription.

At present, the most effective medicinal treatment for childhood anxiety disorder is serotonin-norepinephrine reuptake inhibitors (SNRIs) and selective-serotonin reuptake inhibitors (SSRIs). Other medications include benzodiazepines and tricyclic antidepressants, but these are rarely prescribed for children.

COGNITIVE BEHAVIORAL THERAPY

Cognitive behavioral therapy involves spending time with a mental health professional and talking about your problems. It is designed to get you to change the way you think to enable you to deal with your specific problems. To overcome their anxiety disorder, children are taught how to change negative thinking patterns by identifying them and replacing them with thoughts of a more positive nature. Your child is also taught the difference between realistic and unrealistic thoughts. After each session, the therapist will assign them tasks to complete at home to assist them in becoming more actively engaged in their treatment.

It goes without saying that supporting your child through this process will improve the chances of successful treatment. This involves getting the whole family and the school involved to ensure everyone is on the same page.

Your child will have a limited number of CBT sessions; they typically last for 12 weeks, but the skills they learn during this time will equip them for a lifetime. You will need to consult your insurance provider to determine whether CBT is covered, and they are likely to have a list of therapists to refer you to.

ACCEPTANCE AND COMMITMENT THERAPY (ACT)

Acceptance and commitment therapy is different from CBT in that instead of challenging negative thoughts, it teaches children to accept their thoughts, but to then diffuse them using techniques such as mindfulness, language and metaphors.

The main aim of ACT is to help people understand that attempting to eliminate pain and distress from our lives is a pointless endeavour, as this intensifies the problem, and will ultimately lead to something of a more serious nature. Nevertheless, this does not mean that suffering or defeat is welcomed. Instead, there is an acknowledgement that these experiences are allowed. Space is given to negative sensations, thoughts and feelings, allowing them to come and go without resisting them.

GETTING THE RIGHT HELP

Mental health is just as important as physical health, and if you suspect your child is suffering from an anxiety disorder, book an appointment with your doctor immediately. However, it is also important you find a healthcare professional that you and your child feel comfortable with.

There are many mental health professionals qualified to administer treatment for anxiety disorders. Nurse practitioners and psychiatrists can prescribe medication. Counselors, social workers and psychologists will have training in cognitive behavioral therapy and other talk therapies.

QUESTIONS TO ASK POTENTIAL THERAPISTS

Once your doctor has recommended a few therapists, you will want to know as much about them as possible before going ahead and making an appointment. Here are some questions to ask to help you make the right decision:

- What qualifications/training/experience do you have in treating childhood anxiety disorders?
- What age groups do you specialize in treating?
- Do you have training in specific therapies?
- How do you typically approach treatment?
- If you determine that my child needs medication, will you be able to prescribe it? If not, can you refer me to someone who can?
- How long does treatment typically last in terms of weeks or months?
- How often are the treatment sessions held and what are the time slots for each one?
- Are family members allowed to be present in sessions?
- What signs should I look for to indicate that my child is getting better?
- When do you decide to modify or change the treatment if it seems that my child is not responding to it?
- How much should I tell my child's school about his/her anxiety disorder?

- What is your strategy for discussing drug and alcohol abuse with teenagers who take medication?
- Will you interact with my child's pediatrician or doctor about their treatment?
- How often will I need to make a payment? Do you have payment plans? What happens if I get into financial difficulty?
- Do you accept health insurance?

If a therapist is hesitant or uncomfortable with answering your questions, or your child is not at ease with them, it is best that you continue with your search.

How to Detect Anxiety in Your Child

Sensitive children find it difficult to express their emotions; when they are feeling overwhelmed with anxiety, it is not uncommon for them to retreat and draw back or act out in uncharacteristic ways. It is essential that you know when your child is struggling with anxiety; most importantly, because they themselves do not know how to articulate it.

Physical sensations are one of the most common manifestations indicating that your child is feeling anxious; these include:

- Hair pulling, picking skin
- Diarrhea, stomach ache, cramping, nausea
- Palpitations, chest pain, difficulty breathing
- Constant coughing, dry mouth, difficulty swallowing
- Nightmares, sleep interruptions, restlessness, dizziness, headaches

You should also look out for the following types of behavior:

- Restlessness and agitation
- Feeling out of control, angry outbursts
- Constantly thinking negative thoughts
- Feeling tired, not being as active, wanting to hide

It is important to note that these symptoms could be the result of an unrelated medical condition, therefore, if your child is experiencing any of them, it is essential that you take him/her to a doctor to get a proper diagnosis. However, they can also be signs of anxiety and so you will need to engage with your child to find out how they are feeling.

HOW TO ENGAGE WITH A CHILD SUFFERING FROM ANXIETY

It will become apparent that your child is suffering from anxiety once they get the chance to reflect on how they are feeling, but you will need to help them with this in a calm, slow and patient way. Here are some questions that will help them connect with what's going on inside:

- When did you first start feeling this way?
- Do you remember what was going on when you first started feeling this way?
- Have you ever felt this way before?
- When you felt this way before, what did you do to make the feeling go away?

Children typically get relief from anxiety when they understand the physiological symptoms associated with the attack, such as a nauseous feeling before they have to do a presentation in front of the class, or butterflies in their tummy before an exam. Having an open conversation in which the adult expresses empathy by telling stories of similar experiences will help the child feel less afraid about what they are going through, which will help reduce the symptoms.

How to Reduce Anxiety in Children

There are specific strategies you can implement that will assist your child in dealing with anxiety. It is important to understand that anxiety won't magically disappear, but these strategies will help your child manage the condition when it shows up. Some of these exercises are age sensitive, and it is unlikely that a three-year-old will be able to take part in creative visualization. However, you know what your child is capable of, so choose the exercises you know they will be most comfortable with.

- **Stay Calm:** The first step is to remain calm; children learn by what they see and not what they hear. If you get upset about them getting anxious, it will only make their anxiety worse. When children fall over, the first thing they do is look at their parents and base their reaction on how they act. If the mother or father panics, the child is more likely to start crying. Children tap into their parents' emotions and align themselves with them. If your child picks up on your anxiety about the situation, it will intensify theirs. It is difficult not to worry when your child is going through something traumatic, however, if you are unable to remain calm, you will ultimately make things worse for your child. It will take being intentional about this, so you may need to do some breathing exercises, and ensure that your facial expression does not display worry.

- **Educate:** Spend time teaching your children about the nature of worry. Explain that it is normal for people to feel anxious, and when they do, they experience different feelings in the body and the mind. Children panic when they get anxious because they don't know what's going on, but once they understand it, the less anxious they will be.

- **Breathing Exercises:** Breathing exercises are a great way to reduce anxiety. There are a number of different types you can get your child to practice.

Paced breathing: This technique reduces stress in the body by activating the mechanisms responsible for stress reduction.

- Take a deep breath for 2-4 seconds and then breathe out for 4-6 seconds.
- Focus the attention on a certain sound, image, object or the breath to distract the mind.
- Take a few normal breaths, and then a deep breath.
- Breathe in slowly through the nose and allow the lower belly and the chest to expand.
- Purse the lips and breathe out slowly through the mouth and make a swooshing sound.
- If the mind starts wandering, focus on the breathing or start counting.

- Repeat for up to 10 minutes or until the anxiety subsides.

Abdominal Breathing: This technique will help your child feel calm, renew their energy and give them focus.

- Sit in a chair and place one hand on the stomach and the other on the chest.

- Breathe deeply through the nose.
- Purse the lips and exhale through the mouth.
- Repeat for up to 10 minutes or until the anxiety subsides.

4-4-8 Breathing: This breathing exercise helps reduce tension and stress because it clears the mind and calms the nervous system.

- While sitting down, take a deep breath through the nose for 4 seconds. The breath should go all the way down into the stomach.
- Hold the breath for 4 seconds.
- Breathe out through the mouth for 8 seconds.
- Repeat this 3-4 times, or as many times is required until the anxiety subsides.
- **Mandala Circles:** Most children like drawing, so this is an effective way to get them to focus on the activity instead of their anxiety. The technique helps calm the mind. Give your child a pencil and paper and sit them down in a quiet place, ask them to draw a large circle and fill it with whatever they like. The catch is that they cannot let the pencil leave the paper unless they are changing colors. Allow your child to continue this for 10 minutes.
- **Creative Visualization:** This technique involves thinking about a situation, place or scene where you feel restful, happy and safe. Get your child to sit in a comfortable position, close his or her eyes, and gently breathe through the nose. Ask them to imagine the place in their mind, to use all their senses to taste, touch and hear what is going on in their imaginary environment. Allow your child to continue this for 10 minutes.

- **Problem Resolution:** Once your child has pinpointed their emotions, and they feel that you understand what they are going through and you are willing to listen, work with your child to help them solve their problem. Don't resolve the issue for them. Instead, encourage them to come up with a list of solutions. If they are mature enough to think about their own solutions, that's fantastic, but if not, make a list of potential solutions, ask them to choose the one they think is the most suitable and get your child to articulate why they think it will be the most effective way to solve the problem.

- **Give Your Child Freedom of Expression:** Some parents want their children to grow into warriors. I experienced this in my own household where I was not given the freedom to express negative emotions. If I told my parents I was scared, they would say something like, *"Fear doesn't live in this house, you are not scared."* It wasn't long before I learned to keep my emotions to myself, and ultimately, that had a detrimental effect on my mental health. You want your children to feel they can speak to you about anything. Validate their emotions by saying you can sense their fear. Gently ask what they are worried about and then have a conversation about their fears and emotions.

- **A Good Night-time Routine:** Make sure your child goes to bed at the same time every night whether they are in school or not. Around 30 to 40 minutes before they go to sleep, start a routine to help them get into a relaxed state. Not only will a night-time routine give your child stability, it will increase the chances of them sleeping throughout the night (see Chapter 9 for more details on bedtime routines).

- **Reward Brave Behavior:** Be careful with this one because you don't want to encourage your child to act brave just to get a reward. However, it is a great way of getting him/her to confront their fears instead of running away from them. Anytime your child successfully challenges their anxiety, reward them with something. You can start with praise and then give them a small treat like a sticker or a toy, or you can allow them to watch TV for longer than normal. Eventually, your child will initiate this behavior because they are looking forward to the reward.

- **Be an Example:** As mentioned, children learn from what they see and not what they hear. There is no point in encouraging your child to overcome their anxiety if you do not practice what you preach. We all have fears and anxiety, but it is important that we don't allow them to control our lives. Whenever you are confronted with something you are afraid of, let your child witness you confronting it. If you take the time out to care for your own needs, your child will learn that self-care is important. When you are facing a negative situation, look at the positive side of things instead of focusing on the problem. Remember, your child's psychological well-being is dependent upon yours, and this is something you will need to think about when you are supporting your child through their anxiety.

- **Schedule Time to Have Fun:** Some parents are too hard on their children and even playtime can turn into a performance circus. Allow your children to be children, schedule time for them to play and have fun without having to compete.

- **Focus on the Positives:** Stressed and anxious children can consume themselves with negative thinking and find it difficult to navigate their way out. They might spend time worrying about an upcoming event or something else that's concerning them. Once you have identified the problem and your child understands why they are feeling this way, get them to focus on the positive aspects of the situation instead of on all the things that could go wrong.

- **Embrace Imperfection:** A lot of anxious children worry that they will never be good enough and they are constantly trying to achieve perfection. Start by asking your child why they want to be perfect, and then remind them that there is nothing wrong with being imperfect; as long as he/she has tried their best, it is okay to make mistakes and have flaws.

- **Face Their Fears:** When we are afraid of something, we avoid it, and this is a natural human reaction. However, avoidance only makes it worse; when a child is able to face their fears, they will learn that anxiety is not permanent and after a while, it wears off because the body naturally calms itself down. When you remain in the anxiety-provoking situation for 20-45 minutes, the anxiety will subside.

CHAPTER 4:

DIET AND HOW IT AFFECTS EMPATH CHILDREN

The food sensitive children eat will affect their mood and behavior. We all know that sweets cause hyperactivity. But what is less obvious is that there are other mood-altering foods that you may be feeding your child.

Food Allergens: When a child is intolerant or allergic to certain foods, it can cause behavioral and health issues. Common food allergens include corn, soy, eggs, nuts and dairy products. Without the assistance of a professional food allergist, it can be difficult to determine what foods are making your child sick. It is not uncommon for children to be diagnosed with ADHD when a food allergen goes undetected.

Preservatives: A lot of foods are laced with preservatives, and many of them can cause behavioral problems in children. These include, but are not limited to, monosodium glutamate (MSG), sodium benzoate and nitrites, all of which are known to cause mood alterations, hyperactivity and headaches. You will find sodium benzoate in juice products, MSG in fast foods (especially Chinese) and nitrate in processed meats.

Sugar: It is well known that sugar causes hyperactivity in children. Unfortunately, sugar is found in the majority of foods and the only way to avoid it is through a whole-foods diet. Studies reveal that sugar is linked to sleep problems, cognitive delay and depression.

Artificial Coloring: Artificial coloring has been banned in several countries because it has been linked to a number of physical and mental health conditions in children such as hyperactivity, anxiety, ADHD and headaches. Artificial coloring is often one of the harmful ingredients present in sugary foods and so parents will unknowingly blame any changes in behavior on sugar. Artificial coloring is hidden in foods such as yogurt and bread which are not foods the average person would be suspicious of.

Dairy: Some children are allergic to the protein in dairy, or are lactose intolerant. As a result, they can become aggressive, cranky or irritable. Children with dairy intolerance or allergies are prone to ear infections and colds.

IS YOUR CHILD A PICKY EATER?

There is nothing wrong with having a preference for certain foods; there are some things that I definitely can't eat. Assertiveness is good, it's okay to know what you want. However, there are some children who will refuse to eat anything apart from apples and baked beans, or they will only eat chocolate buttons. This is often because they are highly sensitive.

With heightened flavors, temperatures, textures and aromas that affect the palate, eating affects the senses. Eating is also something that we need to do to stay alive, and it is attached to several emotional responses. One of the reasons why we enjoy eating with our nearest and dearest is that it has the ability to make us feel vulnerable.

LOOKING THROUGH THE HSP LENS

When it comes to picky eating, understanding your child through the HSP lens is essential. This is not to say that all highly sensitive children are fussy eaters, but it has been determined that some of them are. Here are some things you might want to consider:

- **Consistency:** Empath children can be sensitive to certain consistencies and textures. Foods that are not blended properly, are too smooth, undercooked, or mushy, may cause your child to react on a sensory level. Get your child to talk about the consistency of the food by asking them questions about it.

- **Flavor:** Does your child have a preference for bland food? For example, they might like eating potatoes, rice or pasta with no sauce, or toast with no butter. Their heightened sensitivity causes them to react this way. Is your child always covering his/her nose when they are eating? This is how they protect themselves against the intensity they are experiencing. In one study conducted by Professor Linda Bartoshuck from the University of Florida, it was discovered that there are some people who experience food a lot more intensely than others because they have overly sensitive taste receptors. These participants were referred to as 'super tasters.'

HOW TO HELP YOUR EMPATH CHILD ENJOY THEIR FOOD

So now you know your child's picky eating is due to their sensitivity, the question is what can you do to get them to enjoy their food more?

Work with Their Senses: Many parents make the mistake of trying to force their children to eat certain foods because they assume their child is just being rebellious. You can start by working with your child to find out what they don't like about the food. You can do this by going through all the senses.

Smell: Smell your child's food and then get them to smell it; you can then have a discussion about what the smell reminds you of. Start with their favorite smells first, because there is a chance that smells they don't like can trigger negative emotions.

Sight: Talk about what the food looks like; do the colors invoke a certain feeling or emotion in your child? You might find out that they like the way green vegetables look because it reminds them of grass, and they love playing on the grass. They might not like yellow food because it reminds them of bumble bees, and they are not fond of them.

Textures: Does your child prefer their food to be a certain texture? Maybe they don't like foods that feel slimy or runny. Take the time to dissect the meal with your child; do things like cutting, mashing, mixing and stirring and see how they react to this.

COOK TOGETHER

Getting your child involved in the meal preparation process will not only encourage them to enjoy their food; they are also learning a valuable skill that will prepare them for adulthood. It is essential that children learn how to cook from a young age so when they are older and they move out, they can fend for themselves. Additionally, cooking is a great way to bond with your children because it's loving, practical and experiential. It is also a way of showing them that they have a choice; that if they don't like something, they don't have to cook it.

Get Expert Advice

It's not only frustrating when your child is a picky eater, it's also worrying. A child who only eats certain foods is being deprived of the essential nutrients they need to grow and develop. A specialist will help guide you in the right direction concerning your child's diet.

CHAPTER 5:

UNDERSTANDING ANGER IN EMPATH CHILDREN

Anger is an important subject for highly sensitive children. It is essential that this emotion in HSCs is properly understood because there is a tendency to misdiagnose them with behavioral disorders due to the intensity of their outbursts. In most cases, you will have observed that your empath child can switch from calm to completely out of control for apparently no reason. They fly off the handle at things that the average child would brush off as a joke. This is because they feel their emotions on a much deeper level. Other emotional outbursts are much easier to handle than anger, and parents of HSCs often find their behavior very difficult to cope with. In this chapter, you are going to learn about the things that typically make empath children angry, and strategies to help parents deal with this emotion more effectively.

ANGER - WHAT CAUSES IT?

Highly sensitive children are known to hide their emotions either because they don't know how to express them, or because they are ridiculed or punished for them. As a result, they have a lot of pent-up frustration; so oftentimes, when they are acting out, it's not because Sally took the toy they wanted to play with. When your child has an outburst, you've got to scratch beneath the surface to find out what's really going on. It helps to view your child's anger as an iceberg; you can only see the tip of an iceberg, while the majority of it is hidden beneath the sea. In other words, anger is just an expression of the real emotions they have buried.

The normal reaction of any parent when their child is having a temper tantrum is to scream right back in an attempt to get them under control. As the parent of an empath child, you are probably aware that this is the worst thing you can do. Your first reaction should be to try and work out what other emotion is causing your child to act in this way. Do they feel disrespected? Nervous? Frustrated? Overwhelmed?

Anxiety is one of the main causes of anger in highly sensitive children. When a child doesn't feel comfortable in a social situation, or they have worries and fears they don't know how to express, they suppress them, and eventually those feelings resurface as anger.

PAY ATTENTION TO REPETITIVE BEHAVIOR

Since most of you reading this are not psychologists, you are going to find it difficult to work out the underlying emotions causing your child to have angry outbursts. Therefore, pay attention to the occasions when your child has an outburst; is it before dinner? Before school? Before going to a certain person's house? Does it appear to be a normal occurrence when they are with a certain sibling? Does it happen when they are doing homework and can't figure stuff out?

Pay attention to your child's behavior and write everything down, even if it doesn't seem relevant. There could be several things that are causing your highly sensitive child to have angry outbursts. Taking note of these emotions will help you spot repetitive behavior, which will ultimately help you find a solution. Here are a few scenarios you might recognize:

Angry Outbursts Before School: Does your child have an outburst for example every Thursday morning before school? Maybe there's an activity taking place they don't like. If they have suddenly started having outbursts every morning, it might be because they have had a falling out with a friend, or they don't feel comfortable with one of their new teachers. Maybe a new activity is overly stimulating for them.

Angry Outbursts When Playing with Siblings: It could be that one of their siblings is a bit loud, or they have a heavy hand during playtime. Maybe the brother or sister is very competitive, and they struggle with jealousy?

Outbursts When They Are Struggling: The struggle could be with anything; they might find it difficult to learn a new skill or play a game. Maybe they can't solve a math problem, or they are finding it hard to articulate their thoughts when writing something.

How to Help Your Child Overcome Anger

If adults find it difficult to control their anger, children are not going to be any better at it. So it's up to you as a parent or a caregiver to give your child the tools to help them deal with this intense emotion.

It Starts with You: Children are more concerned with what you do than with what you say. Do you hold in your emotions and then have an angry outburst over something seemingly insignificant? Or do you have a bad temper in general? If so, your child is going to pick up on this and assume it's normal to have angry outbursts. Additionally, your child's anger can act as a trigger, and your initial reaction might be to get angry when they do. If you are also a highly sensitive person, you may even take it personally when your child gets angry. With that being said, it is essential that you stay calm during an outburst. You are not going to master this skill overnight, especially if you have become accustomed to reacting with anger. It sounds cliché, but it's impossible to fight fire with fire; you've got to become the water for the blaze.

Punishment: Most parents are going to want to drag their child into their room and lock the door when they are having an outburst. It might seem like the right thing to do at the time, but it is not a good idea. In the long run, your child will feel as if they are being punished for having feelings which will make the situation a lot worse. You will end up in a vicious cycle, and your child's outbursts will escalate because they can't express how they really feel, and you will get even angrier as a result. After a lengthy screaming match in which you've both said things you didn't mean, you will eventually calm down and apologize. But two days later, you are back to square one. This doesn't mean you let them get away with bad behavior; you've just got to deliver consequences at the right time.

Cool-Down Time: You will both need time to cool down because, as you already know, you can't get anything accomplished with two angry people. As long as your child has not become violent, or verbally abusive, allow them to feel angry and give them the chance to cool down before speaking to them. If you are at home, you can let them go to their calm space. If you are out, take your child somewhere quiet and away from everyone else.

Show Empathy: Sensitive children don't react well when they feel they are not understood. A frustrated and angry person is not in the right frame of mind to have a conversation. Instead of bombarding them with shame and judgment, wait for your child to calm down and let them know you are there when they are ready to talk. No matter how ridiculous it seems to you, what your child is feeling is very real to them and they want to be around someone who understands what they are going through.

Name Their Feelings: After everything has settled down, the situation has cooled and your child has calmed down enough to talk, give their feelings a name by saying something like, *"I understand you are feeling angry at the moment,"* or, *"I can see not being able to work out that math problem made you very frustrated."* By giving their feelings a label, you are teaching them how to identify and name their feelings, so they are better able to communicate them in future.

Younger children will benefit from using feelings cards or a feelings wheel. They show a range of emotions and are very useful for helping kids give a better explanation of their feelings. As your child gets older, identifying his/her feelings through drawing and writing also works very well. If you are the creative type, you can make these resources yourself or you can purchase them online.

Identifying Triggers: It's equally as important for you and your child to be able to identify their triggers. If your HSC is old enough to talk about what they think made them angry, you can have a conversation about it. Go back to your journal and discuss patterns that you've noticed. Do they have outbursts before or after school, when they are overwhelmed, tired, hungry, or when they feel they are being ignored or losing a game? When discussing these points, listen to your child's opinion. It will give you better insight into what's going on and help you move forward.

Make a Plan: After your discussion, you will both be in a better position to put a plan in place to manage outbursts effectively. Start by discussing what your child can do when he/she starts feeling angry. What help will they need to control and deal with their feelings better? What calming methods work best? And how can they feel more confident about controlling their anger?

Self-Esteem and Relationships: In general, children need to feel valued and loved, but highly sensitive children need to feel this way even more. Furthermore, deep down, HSCs know there is something different about them which can make them feel extremely insecure. Spend time connecting with your child daily, let them know how much they are loved, and that your love for them is unconditional.

Providing your child with the right tools to help them manage their anger and frustration is essential. It can be one of the most difficult things to do, but it is also one of the most important. Dealing with anger management is not something you want to ignore because as mentioned, empath children are often misdiagnosed with some type of behavioral disorder. This can lead to them being put on medication they don't really need. Unfortunately, some parents go down the medicinal route because it's easier for them. A medicated child will have fewer outbursts, but the long-term consequences can be devastating. Getting over this hurdle is not going to be immediate, but it is possible. Perseverance and consistency are the key.

The Difference Between a Sensory Meltdown and a Tantrum

The reality is that children are manipulative and will often throw a tantrum because they know it will get them what they want. But in some cases, an empath child is not having a tantrum but a sensory meltdown. It's important you know the difference between the two and how to handle them. Let's start by defining them:

What is a Tantrum?

Small children express their frustrations through tantrums that take place because they don't have the vocabulary or the emotional maturity to articulate how they are feeling. Tantrums are typically a reaction to not getting their own way. They either don't like something they've been given, or they are acting out because of something they want. Hungry or tired children are also known to act out in this way. Additionally, there are some situations that will automatically lead to a tantrum, such as not wanting to go to bed, having to leave a place when they are having fun, being told to share their favorite toy or being told to eat something they don't like.

Most tantrums are resolved by giving the child what they want. However, this temporary solution is a bad idea and will ultimately lead to spoiled child behavior in future. Nevertheless, in situations where the child is tired or hungry, giving them a snack or putting them down for a nap is okay.

What is a Sensory Meltdown?

When a highly sensitive child feels overwhelmed because of sensory overload, it is normal for them to have a meltdown. This overload might build up over time, or it can happen all at once. There are a range of factors that will determine your child's tolerance level. A sensory meltdown is different from a tantrum because the child isn't acting out about something they want or didn't get. Most children don't have sensory meltdowns in the home, rather they take place when they are in places with a lot of sensory input to the point of overload.

For example, you are out running errands with your child, you've been to three different stores and everything seems fine. Before you get out of the car, you let your son/daughter know that this is the last store you are going into. But as soon as you step through the front door, they start acting up. What happened?

Are there too many people in the store? Is the music too loud? Are there bright lights flashing? A normal child can block out this type of sensory output, and it won't affect them at all, but this is not the case for highly sensitive children. Try and put yourself in your child's shoes for a moment and imagine a situation that overwhelms you. For me, I don't like fast amusement rides, and since I have full knowledge of why I don't like them and the negative feelings I experience when I get on them, I avoid them. The way you feel when you get on a fast amusement ride is how your child feels when they are experiencing sensory overload. The only difference is that they don't know why they feel like this, how to communicate those feelings, or how to shut those feelings out. The only way they know how to release those feelings is by having a sensory meltdown.

Pay Attention to Limitations: Children have minimal control over their lives; they are told what to do and when to do it at all times. As parents, it's essential you are in tune with your child's sensory limits and emotional needs. For example, if you know your child finds it difficult to cope in crowded places, or in places where there are a lot of smells, plan ahead and don't take them there. If they are invited somewhere by school friends, find out from the parents about the location. If you have time, go and visit on your own to ensure you are not putting your child in a position where they are going to feel uncomfortable.

The only way to relieve your child when they are having a sensory meltdown is to remove them from the situation.

What is Causing the Behavior?

The next step is to understand the driving force behind your child's behavior. Their triggers and personality type are usually the biggest indicators. As mentioned earlier, it helps to pay attention to repetitive behavior, as this will help you determine whether your child is having a sensory meltdown or a tantrum. Is your child the life of the party or do they have a hard time at special events and celebrations? Do they transition well into new situations or do they find it difficult? Does your child start acting up when they don't get what they want, or do they have random emotional outbursts? As you take note of your child's behavior, you will start noticing patterns.

Sensory Meltdown or Tantrum?

Now you are armed with this information, you've got to decide whether your child is having a sensory meltdown or a tantrum so you can act accordingly – and sometimes it's difficult to tell the difference. You need to understand your child and carefully examine the situation before choosing how to respond. For example, if your child is trying to do or reach for something they've been told is off limits, there is a good chance they are having a tantrum.

Did the outburst seem to happen for no reason? Did your child suddenly start covering their eyes or ears? Have you been out running errands for too long and they prefer to be in the comfort of their own home? In such cases, they are likely to be having a sensory meltdown.

Is it time for them to take a nap, or have they not eaten in a while? They are probably having a tantrum.

Sensory meltdowns and tantrums require very different responses which is why it's essential you know the difference between the two.

CHAPTER 6:

EMPATH CHILDREN AND GENTLE DISCIPLINE

Raising a sensitive child is frustrating. They cry and get emotional at the slightest hint of aggression, and so to avoid sending them into a spin, some parents of empath children allow them to 'get away with murder.' It is difficult to teach HSCs about consequences, boundaries and limits when you are dealing with such intense emotions. You have probably read every parenting book out there and sought advice from your well-meaning friends and family members, but nothing seems to work. This is a tricky dilemma, because you understand that, while your child is highly sensitive, they need discipline or there is a good chance they will grow up to be terrible teenagers and adults.

One of the worst aspects of having an empath child is that other people don't understand. Their friend's parents will often get fed up with them and politely inform you that they are no longer welcome at their home. It's not that they are bad children, they are just overly sensitive and another adult who doesn't understand this will apply harsh discipline methods in an attempt to get them in line, and that can have a devastating effect on them.

The good news is that it is possible to discipline your HSC, you've just got to take a different approach than traditional methods. Before you delve into this chapter, understand that, because you are stepping outside the box, you can expect some backlash from your nearest and dearest. They will accuse you of spoiling the child and argue that you are going about things the wrong way, because that's not how *they* would go about it. But they are not directly dealing with highly sensitive children so it's not something they will understand. It's imperative that you stand your ground because your child's well-being is at stake.

HAVE A CALM AREA

A common discipline strategy for parents when their children start acting up is to put them in 'time out,' or make them sit on the 'naughty chair.' This involves either having a designated spot to send the child during an outburst, or creating an impromptu set-up, regardless of the location. This strategy will not work with a highly sensitive child because it will scare them and make the situation a lot worse. If you have tried this method, you are probably well aware of how ineffective it is. So what's the solution? Create a calm area instead.

A calm area is a place where your child can wind down and reconnect with their emotions. The 'time out' area, on the other hand, may be seen as a place of punishment because too often, empath children are punished for being who they are. Their 'overreactions' are seen as disobedience, when in fact, they are having a natural reaction to something they have encountered. It's not their fault they are highly sensitive. So when parents make them sit on a naughty chair, or sit in time out, the message they are sending them is, *"It's not okay to be emotional, you need to hide your authentic self."* Once this notion has been internalized, it becomes another psychological issue empath children carry with them into adulthood.

The calm area should feel welcoming to the child and it should be a place they want to go. You will never catch a child volunteering to go to a time out spot or sit in a naughty chair. But once your child understands what a calm area represents, they will make their way there when they start feeling things are getting out of control. Put things in that area that make your child feel at ease. This might include coloring books, weighted blankets, activity books or books to read. Watching your child get overly emotional about something seemingly irrelevant can become an irritant. So you should also use their calm area time to ground and center yourself and get in touch with your emotions, as this will enable you to communicate more effectively with your child.

You are not always going to be at home when your HSC starts acting up… you might be at a friend or relative's house, or at the store. During these times, calmly remove your child from the situation, and whatever you've got to say, don't say it in front of others. When a highly sensitive child gets embarrassed, they get even more emotional. It is also important that you remain calm because your child will have already picked up on the displeasing energy of others. You know those stares you get when your child is having a tantrum and everyone is looking thinking, *"Can't she keep her child under control?"* Normal children don't care about such attention; in fact, they thrive on it. Highly sensitive children are different, and if you want to bring them back into balance, you will need to do your very best to control your emotions.

YOUR VOLUME AND TONE OF VOICE

It is only natural to want to lash out when your children are acting inappropriately. Some parents don't give their volume and tone of voice a second thought and will yell and scream their young ones into submission. A loud voice and aggressive tone will scare an empath child and cause them to become even more upset. The average parent is not going to feel comfortable with this behavior though, and they will feel as if they are allowing their child to control them. But since your child is not an average child, you are not an average parent, and for the sake of the emotional well-being and stability of your child, you will need to make the necessary compromises. Before approaching your child, take a few seconds (or however long it takes), to regain your composure. Your voice should be firm but calm, so your child knows their behavior is not okay, as well as what to expect from you.

MAKE YOUR EXPECTATIONS AND CONSEQUENCES CLEAR

Highly sensitive children like to know exactly what's going on around them, as they are not comfortable with uncertainty. When they have boundaries and they know what to expect, HSCs are in their element. Following rules is natural to them, so if you let them know what you expect, they will have no problem falling into line. Get into a routine of sitting down together as a family and going over the rules and expectations, and the consequences of disobedience.

If you are going out, once you arrive at your destination, remind your child how you expect them to behave. Do this before getting out of the car so it's not said in front of others. Once you have said what needs to be said, get your child to repeat it so you know he/she understands. By using this strategy, you will greatly decrease your chances of an outburst in public.

Get on the Same Level and Provide Options

How would you feel if you were sitting down and your partner stood over you yelling? Intimidated and disconnected, right? It's like they are intentionally trying to exert their superiority over you, and it would make you feel very uncomfortable. This is exactly how your highly sensitive child feels when you tower over them and yell.

Instead, when your child steps out of line, kneel down and explain their options. For example, if they are trying to play hide and seek with you when you are cooking, stop what you are doing, kneel down and say something like, *"I know you want to play your favorite game right now, but it's important that I make the dinner so you can have something tasty to eat before bedtime. Shouting at me isn't going to get the dinner made any more quickly. While you are waiting for me to finish cooking, you can go to your room and find a toy you'd like to play with, or you can stay in the kitchen with me and quietly help me with the cooking. If you choose to keep shouting at me, I won't be able to play with you after I've finished. What do you think you would like best?"*

Provide an Empathetic Ear

One of the many mistakes parents make is to shame and judge their children; this is the worst thing you can do to an empath child because they need to feel understood. You should aim to fully understand what your child is dealing with. Once they have spent time in the calm area, and they are ready to talk, they will find it easier to tell you what's going on. Active listening skills are essential when it comes to empathy; don't interrupt your child when they are speaking; he/she will stop speaking once they have said what they want to say. To let them know you've understood, repeat it; you can say something like, *"I understand you feel angry because…"* or *"It makes you upset when…"* Your child will naturally calm down when they feel you are on their side and that you can relate to them.

RE-ESTABLISH YOUR RELATIONSHIP

Empaths hate it when they feel they've hurt someone's feelings and they are quick to apologize if they think they have done so. They are also more comfortable following rules than breaking them and will feel extremely guilty when they do. To prevent your child from having an emotional meltdown after they have been disciplined, it's important that you take time out to reassure your child, hug and praise them for the things you appreciate about their character, and let them know they are loved. Sensitive children process things on a deeper level which is why they need additional positive reinforcement and attention after the correction process.

PRACTICE MAKES PERFECT

You are not going to get this right the first time around; it is difficult to discipline children as it is. Some things work, and others don't, which is why you will need to try different approaches and see which is most effective. After finding what works for you, stick to it. There is a high likelihood you are not used to this type of discipline as this is not how you were raised. Parents tend to discipline their children according to how they were disciplined, but you are dealing with an empath child, so you will need to make a lot of adjustments. Don't be too hard on yourself if things don't work out immediately, or you find yourself slipping back into old habits. Remember, it is going to take a while. You will also need to adjust the discipline strategies as your child gets older. The same things that worked when your son or daughter was six probably won't work when they are 13.

Unfortunately, as with all children, you will have plenty of opportunities to practice your newfound discipline strategies. But the good news is that once you have established a routine and you know what works, things will get a lot easier and much less stressful for you.

CHAPTER 7:

HOW EMPATH CHILDREN HANDLE REJECTION

Empath children become terribly overwhelmed when they experience the emotions associated with rejection, isolation or misunderstanding. They find it hard to make sense of and process what has happened. But when these feelings are not understood, parents are unable to give them the help they need to cope. Here are common emotions empath children experience after rejection:

Skinlessness: According to psychologist Gordon Claridge, skinlessness is defined as a hyper-acute sensitivity that manifests in a variety of ways, these include:

- Hyperawareness to sensory stimuli
- Sensitivity to bodily complaints
- Nightmares

Emotional Armor: You will also hear this referred to as 'tough skin.' Emotional armour is what highly sensitive children use to protect themselves against the vulnerability associated with skinlessness. The armor also comes in the form of an alternate personality they use to hide behind so that when the rejection comes, they don't feel it as deeply. The mask comes in the form of refusing to speak, withdrawing, being rude, or acting in a defiant manner. A highly sensitive child might also make themselves look aggressive through their choice of clothes and demeanor. The aim is to become so far removed from their real selves that they no longer feel the pain of rejection.

Emotional armor works in the short term, but the danger is that they become so disconnected from who they really are that they become confused, lost, or feel like a fraud because they are continuously hiding their true selves. Additionally, it leads to loneliness, because in order to form true friendships, authenticity and a real emotional connection is required.

Shutting Down: Highly sensitive children will shut down completely when they are afraid to be themselves or feel misunderstood. The shutting down phase typically starts with wearing emotional armor and with them shutting down all aspects of their personality including their creativity, intuition, deep thoughts and feelings. Shutting down can be an intentional response, but it can also take place as a subconscious reaction to rejection. This is even more dangerous because they are not aware it's happening. An emotional shutdown can also cause the following:

- Numbness
- Frustration
- Lethargy
- Confusion
- Sadness
- Feeling dead inside
- Anger

Frustration, Aggression, Anger: These feelings are the result of feeling socially isolated from being misunderstood and not being able to express themselves the way they would like. Think about it like this: Imagine what it feels like to get told off every time you got genuinely upset because a bird died. Highly sensitive children go through a genuine feeling of grieving when something saddens them. These angry words they hear from adults for not acting like a 'normal' child, and the confusion from not knowing how to process their feelings causes highly sensitive children to feel deeply frustrated and angry, and they tend to internalize this anger. Anger is like a volcano, and when emotional lava reaches the brim, it explodes. When an empath child has a random angry outburst about something minor, it is usually the result of pent-up frustration. Alternatively, these feelings can become so overwhelming, the child reacts by shutting down even further so as not to draw unnecessary attention to themselves.

Feeling Dead Inside, Lethargic, Numb: After lengthy periods of an emotional shutdown, highly sensitive children find it hard to connect with their emotions. During adolescence, the need to release their feelings can manifest through addiction, self-harm, risk taking and adrenaline-releasing experiences. Teenagers like this are often labelled as lazy or apathetic, but the reality is that they have given up on life. It is not something they do consciously; this reaction is subconscious, and they have no idea what is happening to them.

HOW TO HELP EMPATH CHILDREN OVERCOME THESE FEELINGS

The aim is to ensure that your empath child never gets to the stage where they have emotionally shut down. But unfortunately, in some circumstances, you might not realize they are highly sensitive until it's too late.

Resilience: The good news is that when empath children start understanding themselves, and that their personality trait can be challenging for other people in a society that doesn't understand them, they can begin developing a healthy resilience to the negativity and misunderstanding they experience.

Highly Sensitive Friends: One of the heartbreaks highly sensitive children experience is the feeling that they are all alone and no one understands them. This is especially true if they are the only highly sensitive person in the family. Finding highly sensitive friends can be a powerful motivator to help them accept who they are. Life is always easier when you have other people to relate to. As friends, highly sensitive children are able to talk about things they wouldn't be able to with someone who doesn't share their personality.

The Right Environment: In a positive environment where there is understanding and affirmation, empath children develop into confident, strong teenagers and adults. When they are surrounded by people who support and celebrate them, they learn to connect emotionally and enjoy being themselves.

CHAPTER 8:

EMPATH CHILDREN AND BULLYING

C hildren call each other names and tease each other all the time. But highly sensitive children are often victims of bullying because they get emotional over things other children don't pay any attention to. Sometimes, children are not very nice, and can take the teasing and verbal abuse with highly sensitive children too far. It was once believed that physical abuse was worse than mental abuse, but research suggests they are both equally as damaging. This is especially true for empath children.

How Bullying Affects Children

All children can become victims of bullying, and whether they are empaths or not, the effect is usually a negative one. However, due to the nature of their personalities, empath children are easy targets. What's more, because they find it difficult to open up, they are more likely to hide the fact that they are being bullied from their parents. Therefore, it is important to have a clear understanding of how bullying affects children so you can recognize the signs.

Every child is unique and they each have their own gifts, talents and abilities they bring to the world. We live in a society in which it is expected that everyone conforms to the norms and standards that have been established. In other words, we should all fit into a very distinct box, and those who don't are viewed as outcasts. Peer pressure and the herd mentality are prevalent in schools, and the 'outcasts' are seen as a threat to the status quo. It is not uncommon for children (more so teenagers) to conform to the expected standards. But as a result, they feel as if they are hiding who they really are. Therefore, it is essential that parents are intentional about encouraging their children in the areas where they are strong, while not making them feel inadequate about their weaknesses.

Bullying Causes Deep Shame: Bullied children are made to feel like rejects and losers, and they react by internalizing these feelings. This leads to self-hatred, and as the ridicule, mocking and humiliation intensifies, shame is embedded in the subconscious mind. Eventually, this is what drives their behavior.

Bullying Causes Self-Isolation: Self-isolation is an intentional lack of social contact that leads to loneliness. When your child starts self-isolating, they will refuse to engage in social activities, they won't want to go to school and may even pretend they are sick to avoid it.

Bullying Causes Low Self-Esteem: Bullied children lose confidence and begin to doubt themselves. They may feel as if they are not good in certain subjects or a particular activity such as sports, and even if they do participate, they won't make any effort. Bullied children will accept the narrative they are told by their bullies, and as a result, internalize a false concept of self.

Bullying Causes Anxiety: There are several categories of anxiety, including generalized anxiety disorder (GAD), post-traumatic stress disorder (PTSD), and social anxiety disorder (SAD). The stress associated with bullying can cause your child to experience anxiety. Some of the symptoms include a fear of social gatherings, irritability, difficulty concentrating, a sense of dread, restlessness and nightmares.

PRESSURES AND EXPECTATIONS FROM PARENTS

Some parents are just as guilty as playground bullies when it comes to expecting their children to conform to a certain standard. They forget their children are individuals with their own personalities. They want their children to become carbon copies of themselves, or they push their children to become everything they are not. Such pressure confines and limits empath children and often becomes a source of great distress for them. Additionally, it indirectly causes the child to feel ashamed of who they really are. Highly sensitive children are very creative and express themselves in various ways. A child who enjoys dancing will not feel comfortable studying math for hours on end so they can become an engineer like their father. This sense of shame is internalized as they are continuously forced to reject their authentic selves to please their parents.

Putting pressure on a child to conform to a certain standard, whether those standards are being enforced by parents or peers on the playground, will cause long-lasting damage to a highly sensitive child. It is essential that young children and adolescents are encouraged to flourish in their true identity in order for them to grow into confident and self-assured adults. Discovering who we are begins in childhood and it is a life-long process that must be fully encouraged from a young age.

Fear and the Threat Response: In the first two years of life, babies communicate through their emotions. All their interactions and emotional experiences are stored in the right hemisphere of the brain. Despite the fact that bullying is predominantly a form of emotional abuse that involves verbal offenses, it also has an effect on the heart, mind and brain (particularly the right hemisphere). Bullying is social rejection; it causes children to feel overwhelmed and frightened and they are unable to process the experience. When there is a threat present, an internal alarm sets the body into a fight, flight or freeze response that is a survival mechanism that protects us from danger. When children are continuously emotionally overwhelmed, or experience fear without the brain being soothed or calmed, their brain develops into one that is wired on hyper-alert mode because they are always afraid that something bad will happen.

It is crucial that parents and caregivers understand this 'threat response' so they can teach their children that when the body has a physical reaction to emotional trauma it isn't because there is something wrong with them, rather it is a normal human reaction.

The brainstem is an area of the brain located near the back of the neck; this area is fully formed by the time a baby is born. It is connected to the limbic system which is where our emotions are formed. When the limbic system registers a threat, it sends a message to the body that it is in danger, and the response is panic. Hormones are then released to enable the body to react and this reaction is the fight, flight or freeze response. As a result of the threat response, the brain is unable to think rationally. Hence some people turn into superheroes when they are under attack. One well-known story is that of a woman who managed to lift a car off her child. Under normal circumstances, she would have reasoned that there was no way she had the strength to move the weight of a car. But she went into fight mode to protect her child and she was successful.

In this state, all reasoning is lost because there is reduced neural activity in the prefrontal cortex, which is the rational part of the brain. The Broca is another area of the brain that experiences limited functionality when there is a threat present. The Broca is responsible for language and speech. This is why people find it hard to articulate their thoughts when something traumatic happens, and possibly why the term 'at a loss for words' was coined. Further, this is why children often look wide-eyed and shocked, and can't speak when they are scolded.

When children repeatedly experience trauma, they live in a continuous state of fear. They find it difficult to reflect, negotiate, reason or think clearly because those parts of the brain are not operating as they should, due to the stress hormones constantly at work.

RECOVERING FROM FEAR - HOW TO HELP YOUR CHILD

The threat response can have a negative effect on a child's behavior and their ability to connect with people on an emotional level because they don't feel secure. Instead, they feel unstable, confused and scared. Children don't know how to soothe themselves; it is the responsibility of parents to do so. Here are some tips on how to help your child recover from fear:

- **Discuss Their Fears:** As mentioned, one of the reactions to fear is the inability to articulate one's feelings. However, to address their fear, you need to know what has frightened your child. You can do this by gently asking questions about the fear, even if the response is only a yes or no answer. Once your child begins to calm down, they can further explain what has frightened them.

- **Validate Their Fears:** When highly sensitive children are afraid for what appears to be no reason, it is not uncommon for parents to tell them to stop being silly, or to stop being a scaredy cat (this is especially true for boys).

- **Move On:** According to clinical psychologist Dr. Rachel Busman, it is important to move on from the fear once it has been validated. Reinforcing the fear can become a problem, so the idea is to get your child to the point where they are capable of managing the fear by themselves.

- **Set Goals:** Since you want your child to get to the point where they are managing the fear themselves, understand that the only way to achieve this is to set goals. For example, if your child is afraid of the dark and needs you to stay in the room with them until they fall asleep, you could set a goal that for a week: you will sit with them until it's time to turn off the lights, and then they will need to turn off the lights themselves and go to sleep.

- **Be Patient and Provide Encouragement:** Whatever fears your child needs to overcome, success is not going to happen overnight. It is essential that you are patient and provide constant encouragement as they navigate this journey.

CHAPTER 9:

MAKING BEDTIME EASIER FOR EMPATH CHILDREN

After dealing with hyperactive children all day, most parents look forward to bedtime; it's their time to unwind and get things done. Unfortunately, for some highly sensitive children, bedtime is the worst part of the day, and something you would ordinarily look forward to turns out to be a nightmare every evening. The good news is, it doesn't have to be like this. In this chapter, you are going to find out why your HSC hates bedtime, and the strategies you can put in place to put a stop to it.

WHY YOUR CHILD HATES BEDTIME

There are a number of reasons why your child may have a disdain for bedtime. Some children are afraid of being left alone in the dark because their imagination takes over and negative thinking invades them. They still feel overstimulated because they haven't spent enough time unwinding, or maybe they are overtired because they are going to bed too late.

One of the main reasons why highly sensitive children find it difficult to go to sleep is they have very active minds. By bedtime, they are still processing the excitement they've experienced throughout the day. They are also very in touch with their environment and so a sight or a sound that's not familiar can cause your child to overthink and this sets their adrenaline going. So it's not that your child hates bedtime, rather they don't like the feelings associated with it. The following are three strategies that put your child into a relaxed state and help them fall asleep more easily:

Routine: All children need a solid routine, but highly sensitive children need one even more. Good habits and order create a calm environment, so when they know what's coming, they feel safe and are more likely to comply. Young children have no concept of time, but when they get used to a series of events, they will understand that bedtime is drawing near. Here are the elements that make up a good bedtime routine:

- **Timing:** Sensitive children don't like being rushed; it makes them feel overwhelmed. So you will need to start the routine at a decent time to fit everything in. Additionally, HSCs don't like transitioning from one activity to the next because of their tendency to get extremely engrossed in one thing. It's important to start early so they have enough time to spend on each part of the routine. Depending on what you have planned, an hour is generally sufficient to get everything done. Okay, I can already hear you saying, *"An hour! Is that really necessary?"* Think about it like this: when there is no routine in place, it can take hours to get your child to sleep, so spending one hour doing the things that will guarantee your little one falls asleep as soon as the routine is complete is a good payoff. One of the main advantages of a long bedtime routine is that even though your child knows they are getting ready for bed, they are still spending time with you, which increases the likelihood of them cooperating. Adding some fun games that they enjoy will give your child something to look forward to and make the routine even easier.

You also need to think about the time your child goes to sleep. You would assume a tired child would just fall asleep, but exhausted children are prone to meltdowns, making bedtimes all the more difficult. According to author Dr. Elaine Aron, highly sensitive children need more sleep than other children, and so to get enough shut-eye, they should go to bed earlier.

- **Letting Them Choose:** Some parents don't believe in giving their children the power of choice. As far as they are concerned, kids should do as they are told and that's the end of it. However, this is an ineffective way of teaching children how to be independent. Furthermore, when children feel that they are a part of the decision-making process, they are more likely to comply. This is especially true of highly sensitive children because they like to feel in control.

- **Consistency:** The same bedtime routine should take place every night. Skipping a night or two isn't going to work, as this will cause confusion and your child won't know what to expect from day to day. There will be times when it's not possible to have a night-time routine because of an outing or a special event. During these times, it's important to remind your child in advance that there is not going to be a bedtime routine that night because of what's taking place, but they will get back to it the following night. When HSCs know what's coming, there is less chance of them fighting against your authority.

A Relaxing Atmosphere

After getting all the essential tasks out of the way, your next step is to create a relaxing atmosphere that will make it easier for your child to fall asleep. Let your child help you get rid of distractions such as putting toys back into the hamper. Switch off the TV, turn off electronics and dim the lights. Some HSCs enjoy soft music or soothing sounds in the background. These activities will remind your little one that bedtime is drawing near.

The Power of Rituals

The final part of the routine is getting your child into a relaxed state so he/she can fall asleep easily. What you decide to do during this time is up to you and your child. It's a good idea to get him/her involved here, ask them what they'd like to do before going to bed, and provide some suggestions to simplify the decision-making process. Here are a few ideas you might want to consider:

- **Singing:** Remember, the idea is to get your child into a relaxed state, so singing a popular upbeat song isn't going to help. Opt for a soft lullaby instead.

- **Prayers:** This will depend on whether your family is religious, but bedtime is a great opportunity to incorporate prayer into your child's daily routine.

- **Mindfulness and Meditation:** Some activities will depend on the age of your child. If they are old enough, mindfulness and meditation help quiet down the noise from the day.

- **Talk:** Have a discussion about your day. Your child might want to talk about some of the things that are worrying him/her, or about some of the exciting activities that took place during the day. If you have a worry eater, your child can use this time to feed it with their worries. As with all night-time activities, talking can easily turn into a delay tactic to stay awake. So you will need to know when to cut the conversation short.

- **Read:** If your child is of reading age, let them read to you; if not, you can read to them, or you can take turns reading to each other. Reading with children is essential for their development because it improves a child's coping, literacy and language skills. It also provides bonding time between the two of you.

It is important to note that as your child grows, you will need to adapt their bedtime routine, but until they leave your home, always ensure they have a night-time routine. What tends to happen is that parents get too comfortable, and before they know it, they are back to square one. Unless a highly sensitive child has a consistent bed-time routine, both of your sleeping habits will remain inconsistent.

CHAPTER 10:

MOVIES, TELEVISION SHOWS AND EMPATH CHILDREN

Television shows and movies can act as triggers for empath children and it can take a while to figure out what they are. You may have gotten to a point where you think you've figured it out and then something else pops up. Certainly some R rated films can send your child into an emotional meltdown. Sometimes, parents are forced to watch shows in advance to make sure they are appropriate.

Why Are Empaths Affected by What They Watch? Sensitive children notice every detail associated with the information they are exposed to. They absorb every emotion and feeling they are surrounded by. Witnessing someone fall over on TV can have a negative effect on the emotions of an empath because they feel the pain the person is experiencing. They visualize it, or they imagine the same fate happening to them or their loved ones.

If two people are saying an emotional goodbye to each other where tears and feelings of sadness are involved, they will feel this deeply. The child will imagine how it would feel if they had to say goodbye to their loved ones.

Parents should also pay close attention to the commercials in between TV shows, because ads about raising money for homeless people or abused children can trigger a severe emotional reaction and cause an internal battle about the evils of this world.

How Do Movies and TV Shows Affect Empath Children? A reaction can be clear and immediate such as panic, fear, asking to turn off the TV or to leave the cinema. Or your child might sit and cry in silence or go through an emotional withdrawal. When their emotions become too overwhelming, they may manifest physically through a stomach ache, a headache, insomnia or something else. Sometimes, there is no immediate reaction until it's time to go to bed and your child has an emotional meltdown because the lights have been turned off. Additionally, they might go to sleep just fine, but what they saw on TV triggers a nightmare.

When something bad happens on the TV show or movie, the highly sensitive child may end up feeling as if the event actually happened which can lead to a temporary dip in their emotions.

What Can Empath Children Watch? There are plenty of movies and programs they can watch, and at the end of Chapter 12, I have included a list of them. In addition, here are some steps that can help you choose the right material:

- **Watch it First**: As time consuming as this is, watching TV programs and movies beforehand is the best way to determine whether they are appropriate.

- **Read Parental Guides:** Common Sense Media is a great parental guide to read.

- **Join Forums:** If you don't have time to watch a movie or TV show beforehand, join an online forum for highly sensitive parents.

- **Stick to What Works:** 'Variety is the spice of life' doesn't apply to highly sensitive children. When you find something that works, stick with it. However, you can start making incremental changes as they grow older.

GOING TO THE MOVIES WITH EMPATH CHILDREN

Watching a movie at home and watching one in the cinema is an entirely different experience for sensitive children. It is advised that you don't take HSCs to the movies if they are sensitive to light and noise as it can be a sensory minefield for some children. If you are planning on taking an empath child to the movies for the first time, here are some tips to ensure the trip is a success:

Make Sure Your Child is Ready: If your child has a difficult time watching movies at home, it's probably not the right time to take your empath child to the movies.

Content and Age Appropriate: This might seem like a no-brainer, but in most cases, highly sensitive children need to be older than the age stated as appropriate. Unfortunately, we live in a world where it is becoming increasingly common to expose children to scenes of violence and sexually explicit content. What's inappropriate to you is probably not inappropriate to the powers that be making these decisions. It is also a good idea to check some of the parental review sites. Depending on what your child can handle, in some cases, you might just need to warn your HSC about some scenes beforehand.

Length and Pace of the Film: You will also need to consider the length and pace of the movie. Some empath children find it difficult to sit through long ones, and fast paced films can be overwhelming.

When to Enter: The best way to ensure you don't end up having to leave before the film has even started, is to enter the viewing room just as the film is about to start so you miss the trailers about other coming attractions and commercials. There is no way of knowing about the content in a trailer or ad, so to get over this hurdle, just make sure you miss them.

Time of Day: Choose an early show so your child doesn't feel overwhelmed by other things before the movie starts. For example, going to the cinema after school or after going shopping is a bad idea.

CHAPTER 11:

SCHOOL AND EMPATH CHILDREN

School is one of the most important aspects of your child's life, because outside of the home, that is where they will spend the majority of their time. It is essential to their development that they feel comfortable and safe at school. The bottom line is you can't put your child in just any school, no matter how good their reputation is for academic performance. There are many reasons why parents choose a school, and one of them is convenience, such as being located in the local district, or all their friends go there. But with empath children, you can't afford to allow convenience to be your primary deciding factor. Choosing a school is way more complicated for HSCs, and we will get into some of those complications throughout this chapter.

CHANGING SCHOOLS AND EMPATH CHILDREN

Highly sensitive children do not like change; in fact, they hate it! But unfortunately, there are times when you will have no choice but to remove them from school because it is causing them more harm than good. As you will have discovered, the school system makes little room for non-conformists. Children who don't fit into a box are labeled as unruly, and some schools will outright refuse to make allowances for HSCs. But the question is, how will you know when it's time to switch schools or remove them from school altogether and start home-schooling them? Here are some signs that it's time to go:

Meetings Lead to Frustration: Do you leave meetings with teachers feeling worse than when you went in? As far as you are concerned, you might as well have been speaking to a brick wall because no one is listening to you. The teachers are not interested in learning about the unique characteristics of an empath child, they don't want to put in the effort. In their mind, dealing with HSCs is not what they signed up for when they decided to become a teacher.

To make matters worse, you are not going into meetings empty handed. You've got evidence from healthcare professionals, youth services and therapists, and they have even accompanied you to some of your meetings, but that hasn't helped.

You've talked, they've listened and nothing's changed; you don't have anything left to say.

You Don't Trust Your Child's Teachers: It's a big thing leaving your empath child in the hands of someone who doesn't have a full understanding of your child's unique needs. When you've had conversations with teachers, and they agree to certain things like giving your child extra time throughout the day, you leave the meeting feeling relieved that the teacher understands, and satisfied that you've managed to put certain things in place that will make your child more comfortable at school.

But two days after the meeting, your son or daughter comes home crying because they were refused quiet time. You don't want to think the worst, maybe things just got a bit busy at school and quiet time wasn't possible, so you gave it a week and every day, it's the same scenario – tears because there was no quiet time. So, now you have the right not to trust your child's teacher.

Everything you have implemented in the home works, but because they are not implementing it in school, your efforts are being uprooted, and every day it feels like you are starting all over again. When you confront the teacher, they tell you your son/daughter isn't having any behavioral issues and there is no need to give your child any extra help. In other words, you must be lying… your child is not highly sensitive. So now you feel as if you are being mocked.

Does the School Accept the Notion of Empath Children?
Some parents have complained that their child's school doesn't accept the notion of highly sensitive children because there is no scientific evidence to back it up. Since parents cannot provide scientific evidence that highly sensitive children should be treated differently to any other child, they are not going to make any allowances.

In such instances, you will find that teachers don't take children seriously in the classroom when they feel overwhelmed. For example, some empaths get tired when there is too much activity and will need a nap. Your child might tell his/her teacher they need a break, and those requests fall on deaf ears. So your child lays their head down on the table and falls asleep. They are then woken up and told to sit in the naughty chair for falling asleep in class. Incidents like this lead to negative labels being attached to your child.

Eventually, it will become clear that the school is not interested in the well-being of your child. It is not uncommon for schools to accuse the parent of being the problem, implying there must be something going on in the home to cause their child to act like this in school.

Classroom Organization: Initially, you may have been pleased with the way the classroom was organized. The classroom sizes were small, and the children had regular breaks. However, when your child moved up a year, things changed significantly; there were more children and fewer breaks, and your little one started having emotional meltdowns before and after school.

What Are Your Instincts Telling You? Finally, listen to your gut, do your research, have meetings and speak to the right people. But if your instincts are telling you it's time to leave, don't ignore this feeling or you will end up regretting it. Your child's behavior is an indication their instincts are telling them they are not in the right place. They would have felt it long before you did.

THE IDEAL SCHOOL FOR AN EMPATH CHILD

Perhaps the most difficult decision you will make as the parent of an empath child is what school to send them to. If you have more than one HSC, you might have already experienced the turmoil associated with trying to find the right school. Or maybe you have already sent your son or daughter to one school and it didn't work out. Either way, you are going to need some help, so here are some tips to give you an idea of what to look for.

Classroom Size: Empath children don't do well in large groups. Unfortunately, the average size of a classroom in the majority of American schools is 23.1. However, I also understand that you might be reading this in another country and that things are different there. If that's the case, you will need to do some research about class sizes. You need a school that is relatively close because you are probably all too familiar with traveling long distances with a HSC.

Try and stick to classes with around 15 students. But if there isn't one close enough, you will need to compromise.

In general, seating is important for empath children; it's essential they are not seated next to loud or disruptive children. If you can't find a school with small class sizes, perhaps you can request your child be assigned a corner that's somewhat separate from everyone else.

Spaces and Quiet Time: Whether your child is an introvert or an extrovert, downtime is important for highly sensitive children; without it, they find it difficult to function. The reality is that most schools don't have the facilities to fully cater to empath children. But if the school board is willing to compromise, they can make allowances. The ideal school would have the following:

- Space where noise can be shut out, or space where a group of children can make as much noise as they want without it causing a distraction.
- Equipment that masks noise, such as earphones
- A small area where children can unwind
- A comfort space with soft pillows, beanbags and earphones
- Students being given the freedom to work alone when they need to
- A variety of spaces such as designated places for visual stimulation, movement, silence etc.
- A comfortable reading corner
- The permission to recharge when necessary

Children Are Treated as Individuals: Not all children are the same, and some schools fail to recognize this. If students don't conform to a certain standard, it's a problem. Highly sensitive children are unpredictable and don't fit into a box. When teachers know and understand who your child is, they will treat them accordingly. Teachers at an ideal school will:

- Allow parents to sit with their children in the classroom until they are comfortable
- Be willing to spend the time required to get to know their students
- Conduct review sessions in which children interact with the teachers and share how they feel and what they think can be done differently to make their lives better at school
- View children as an extension of the school and not a group of people who are only there to follow the rules

More Than a Teacher: A teacher who truly has a passion for what they do is to be admired and respected. They go above and beyond the call of duty to ensure their students reach their full potential. On the other hand, there are some teachers who only show up for a paycheck and are not at all concerned about the well-being of their students. Once you have shortlisted some schools, set up a meeting with every teacher who would be responsible for your child. Take your child with you, because if your son or daughter doesn't get good vibes from their prospective teachers, you will need to continue your search. It is also important to mention that there are some character traits of a teacher that won't be evident in a meeting. Either way, listen to your instincts. These are some of the most important characteristics you should be looking for:

- A cool-tempered teacher who doesn't shout at students for the smallest infraction
- A teacher who listens to their students and takes what they say seriously

- Teachers who handle the class in a gentle manner
- Teachers who have an understanding of highly sensitive children. If the teacher is highly sensitive that is an added bonus.
- More than one teacher in the classroom at a time
- Teachers who understand mindfulness
- Teachers who are trained to deal with children with a range of personalities
- Teachers who understand the basics of developmental psychology and put them into practice

The School Environment: The look and feel of the classroom is the most important aspect of the school environment because that is where your child is going to spend the majority of their time. You ideally want a classroom environment like this:

- Minimal bright walls
- A cozy environment
- A limited amount of decorations
- Storage for unfinished projects
- Orderly and quiet conditions
- Similar look and feel as a home
- A slow-paced environment

Recess and Breaks: In most schools, things don't slow down during lunch break and recess. Students are typically rushed from one part of the school to another and given a certain amount of time to either eat or play. But this won't work for an empath child; they need time to recharge. The ideal school would allow the following:

- Alone and quiet time during lunch breaks and recess
- Students staying in the classroom and resting during recess

School Hours: Highly sensitive children don't do well with the number of hours they have to spend in school. They get tired and frustrated, and then parents are forced to deal with the aftermath. The ideal school should have the following in terms of hours:

- Fewer hours for a school day than normal
- The ability to home-school during the week
- Flexible school hours

QUESTIONS TO CONSIDER WHEN LOOKING FOR A NEW SCHOOL FOR YOUR EMPATH CHILD

Choosing the right school for your child is challenging, and it will cause you a lot of anxiety, especially if you've already had a bad experience with a current school. The right school is important for all children, but it is even more so for empath children, as it will have a huge influence on their academic and social success. When looking for a new school for your child, asking the right questions is crucial, and it will help you determine whether you are making the right decision. Additionally, you will want to take notes when taking a tour of the school and speak to other parents whose children are students there. You might feel slightly uncomfortable asking so many questions, but you can't afford to be passive during the interview stage. It is important that the school board be aware of how essential the right school is for your child. Here are some questions to consider:

DO YOU HAVE A SUPPORT SYSTEM FOR CHILDREN WITH DIFFERENT ACADEMIC, EMOTIONAL OR SOCIAL CHALLENGES?

When choosing the right school for your child, it is essential that you think ahead. Some empath children have specific sensory sensitivities that could potentially affect their classroom performance.

During the interview stage, make sure you mention these issues, and ask whether they have any guidelines or programs in place to help children work through these challenges. Don't settle for, "Yes, we have plenty of programs…" Get specific, ask them exactly what the programs entail, what their success rates are like, and if you can speak to any parents whose children are a part of these programs.

How many students are there for each teacher?

This teacher/student ratio question is important because you don't want an overwhelmed teacher handling your empath child who also becomes overwhelmed when things get too hectic. Additionally, you don't want to put your HSC in a classroom where there are too many children and there is a good chance the students won't get any 'one-on-one' time.

It's also good to know whether the school uses classroom aides because an extra adult can improve the organization of the classroom. Additionally, depending on the needs of your child, they may feel more comfortable knowing there is extra help at hand if they need it.

Describe the Learning Environment

You know your child's personality and learning style, so you need to know whether the classroom environment will be suitable for them. Does the school focus on using technology as a teaching tool? Is their approach more active and hands-on? Do the students spend the majority of their time working in groups, or do they work independently? Do the children participate in activities where there is a lot of movement? Do the children get to have quiet time?

WHAT TRANSITIONS TAKE PLACE THROUGHOUT THE DAY?

Highly sensitive children don't do well with transitions, especially when they are not aware there is one coming. Therefore, you will want to know how the school structures their day. It takes highly sensitive children a little longer to adjust to a new situation. When the students do have transitions, how long do they get to transition between activities, and are they outside the classroom? What are the timeframes for lunch and recess?

Understandably, transitions are inevitable in schools, but a highly sensitive child will respond better when they know ahead of time that a transition is about to take place. This is even more important at the beginning of the year, but as the year progresses, your son/daughter will get used to the routine.

HOW DOES THE SCHOOL HANDLE DISCIPLINE?

What strategies does the school have in place for challenging behavior? Do they revoke privileges? Do they give detentions? How do they respond to bullying? What policies do they have in place? Do they teach their students about bullying? Are the staff trained to handle bullying?

Empath children have no problems following rules; in fact, they prefer to follow them than break them. They don't like showing their emotions at school, but shouting and strict discipline can have a negative effect on them, even if another student is receiving the punishment.

HOW DO TEACHERS COMMUNICATE WITH PARENTS?

What is the primary method of communication between school staff and parents? Is it letter, email, phone call or text messaging? How often do meetings take place between teachers and parents?

Do parents have direct access to their child's teacher through email, phone or another form of communication? Can parents request meetings with teachers outside of the allotted timeframes?

ARE THERE ANY SPECIALISTS AVAILABLE AT THE SCHOOL?

Some schools have specialists available on site to assist with challenging behavior. These include:

- Occupational therapists
- Speech pathologists
- Social workers
- Psychologists

Depending on the needs of your child, if the school doesn't have any onsite specialists, it's not a deal breaker. However, you should continue your search for a school that does have them if you think there are times your child will need to see a specialist.

INFORMATION TO SHARE WITH YOUR CHILD'S TEACHER

Your child will spend the majority of their time in school, so it's important their teachers are familiar with the peculiarities of your highly sensitive child. This is especially true for young children who have not learned to articulate their feelings in a way that others can understand. To make the best use of your child's time at school, you will need to give their teachers as much information as possible. Additionally, you might want to consider typing out this information into a manual that teachers can have access to at all times. The reality is that schools do not train teachers to deal with empath children, and the majority of them have probably never heard of such a personality type. There is so much information to convey that it's highly unlikely they will remember what is said during a meeting, even if they are taking notes. When it comes to the school environment, there is only so much they are going to do; therefore, it's up to you to become your child's advocate and ensure teachers have access to all the information they need about your son or daughter.

Most teachers are there because they care about children and want to do the best job they can, and will be very open to educating themselves in order to implement the strategies required to give their students the best education possible. Here are some tips to include in your manual:

Your Child's Sensitivities: Do noises, surprises, visual stimuli, or a change in routine cause overstimulation in your child?

Classroom Seating: Highly sensitive children can get frustrated, bothered and distracted by seemingly minor things in the classroom. If things like another child humming to themselves, the sound of a computer, a fly buzzing, the entrance to the classroom, or bright lights cause a negative reaction in your child, the teacher will need to know so he/she can seat your son or daughter appropriately.

Tests and Exams: Some highly sensitive children do not perform well on exams and tests. They find the pressure to do well too stressful and their true potential is often masked by their inability to score high grades. Some highly sensitive children are perfectionists and will analyze a test question from so many different angles that they end up confusing themselves. A good teacher will understand this and will find ways to get the best out of your highly sensitive child. When the teacher knows what to look for, this process becomes a lot easier.

Allowing a child to go for a walk before a test or take some time out for breathing exercises can help highly sensitive children relax before a formal exam.

Tone of Voice: It is the norm for children to push boundaries, and sometimes teachers will need to raise their voice or alter the tone of it to reclaim order in the classroom. But for some empath children, anything other than a soft tone and a calm approach will send them into an emotional meltdown, even if the instructions are not specifically for them. If a teacher needs to address the class, they should explain to your child that they are not in any trouble, but they need to leave the class for a couple of minutes to get things in order. Once the students have settled down, the teacher can then have a quiet word with your son or daughter about what has just taken place and the behavior they need to display moving forwards.

Punishing the Entire Class: Most of the time children are loyal to each other, and if a pupil does something to intentionally disrupt the class when the teacher is not looking, the perpetrator isn't going to own up, nor are any of the other students going to report him or her. In such instances, the teacher is often forced to punish the entire class. Some empath children will take this personally, and the message they will get from it is that they are a bad child. Again, the best way to deal with a situation like this is for the teacher to ask your child to leave the room and then address them separately.

It Takes Empath Children Longer to Adjust: While other children can move from one activity to the next without any problems, highly sensitive children need additional time to adjust after a transition. It is not uncommon for teachers to mistake this behavior as disinterest or apathy, and the typical response is to force the HSC to get involved. Forced participation when they are not ready will cause a highly sensitive child to have an emotional meltdown. This is especially true with new teachers, classes or schools.

Avoid Long Conversations: Because empath children think so deeply, long, drawn-out conversations with a teacher can cause the child to become overwhelmed. They will evaluate every word and sentence to the point of confusion. A teacher who lacks understanding about highly sensitive children won't realize what's happening at the time because your child will internalize their feelings. But it can cause a HSC to become so stressed about school that they get depressed and no longer feel comfortable about going to school. These feelings will typically manifest through a stomach ache or a headache.

Home and School Behavior is Different: In most cases, highly sensitive children feel safe and secure at home, therefore, they feel comfortable acting as themselves. It is not uncommon for a HSC to be reserved and quiet at school, and outgoing, enthusiastic and lively at home. It is important for teachers to understand that they might not get to know your child's true personality.

A Soft Touch: Over-coddling children will do more harm than good. If they don't know where they are going wrong, they can't improve. Constructive criticism is important, but it must be done in a gentle manner or an empath child will retreat because they feel like a failure and will be too scared to try again in case they hear the same negative remarks.

Timing and Reset: When a highly sensitive child gets overstimulated, they can't get back to normal activity unless they have completely calmed down. This usually takes around 20 minutes. This is a long time in a classroom setting, and it could mean that your child misses out on most of the lesson or activity taking place. This is inconvenient for both your child and the teacher, and the only way to avoid it is to ensure your child doesn't get overstimulated in the first place.

Don't Label an Empath Child: Empath children don't jump into conversations right away. They sit back and observe before making a contribution, and in some cases, they might not say anything at all. Teachers often make the mistake of placing labels on children who don't participate by referring to them as withdrawn or shy. Once a highly sensitive child has been labeled, they will conform to that label.

Advance Warning: Although teachers have a set schedule for their students throughout the day, sometimes things don't go according to plan. Highly sensitive children don't deal with change well, especially not sudden change. If the schedule is not going to run normally, give a highly sensitive child advanced warning so they can mentally prepare themselves in advance.

Keep Friends to a Minimum: Empath children are not very confident in social settings and can have a hard time making friends. Additionally, they don't feel comfortable around large groups of people. One close friend who understands their needs is usually enough for an empath child. If a teacher notices that your child spends a lot of time alone, they should help them find a friend they can identify with so they don't feel left out.

Focus on Their Creativity: Highly sensitive children are very creative; they love music, art, dancing and singing. They also have a passion for nature and see the beauty and detail in everything around them.

Trust is Important: Highly sensitive children won't open up if they don't feel they can trust the people around them. A teacher won't know a HSC is struggling because they are hard to read. But when they feel that a teacher is trustworthy, they will feel comfortable sharing when something goes wrong.

Safety and Security: This ties in with empath children being able to trust their teachers. In general, HSCs are not fond of the school environment because they don't feel comfortable. But when they have an adult they can trust and turn to when they start feeling overwhelmed and overburdened, school becomes a lot easier for them.

Praise When Necessary: Highly sensitive children don't respond well to criticism, but when they are praised for a job well done, it encourages them to do better next time.

Break Down Tasks: Classroom assignments and homework can severely overwhelm highly sensitive children when they are not broken down into manageable chunks. If a classroom assignment involves reading a book, making notes and then answering questions relating to the book they've just read, an HSC needs a full explanation of each step. For example, tell them how long they should spend reading the book and what parts to pay attention to in the story so they can answer the questions properly.

Challenge Them: Empath children are usually gifted. They don't take anything at face value, and because they have an accelerated level of understanding, they do things like anticipate the next question after the first question and answer that one instead.

However, their superior level of intelligence is sometimes overlooked because of their inability to concentrate for long periods. Their mind will drift, and they will start focusing on something else. The teacher then assumes the highly sensitive child doesn't understand, but they do; they got it before everyone else in the class and just got bored with the long, drawn-out explanation.

To accommodate highly sensitive children, when a teacher realizes they have understood the explanation, allow them to get on with the task at hand while they explain things further to the rest of the class. In some cases, teachers might need to order additional material like advanced textbooks to keep a highly sensitive child from getting bored.

Their Emotions: Everyone in the work environment knows to leave their personal life at the door before starting their day. But this is especially true with teachers who have empath students because the student will pick up on the teacher's emotions and become distracted and worried. Therefore, it's important that teachers learn how to keep their feelings under control when in a classroom setting.

The Small Things: Getting pushed out of the way on the hallway, a stern word from a teacher or a sly comment from a classmate can send a highly sensitive child into an emotional meltdown. These things won't mean anything to the average child, and they will usually laugh such things off, but not a HSC. When a highly sensitive child gets upset about an incident that doesn't seem like a big deal, it is crucial that teachers don't act dismissively or tell them to stop being silly.

Compassion for Parents: Highly sensitive children prefer to hide their feelings when they are not in a safe place. To a teacher, your child might have had a brilliant day because they sat down quietly and got on with their work. But the negative effects of the day are not unleashed until they get home. Your son or daughter might have an emotional meltdown in the evening, or throw a tantrum in the morning because they don't want to go back to school and experience what they went through the day before. This pattern of behavior can become incredibly frustrating for the parents of highly sensitive children. So it's important that teachers make every effort to enforce the instructions provided in your manual.

Encourage Empath Children to Use Their Insight: Empath children can be a valuable resource in the classroom. They can sense when other students are not in a good place, and their insight into topics they are passionate about can lead to thought-provoking lessons.

Encourage Further Learning: As a parent, you will know a lot about highly sensitive children because of your personal experience and research. However, there are plenty of additional resources teachers can seek out to help them gain a deeper understanding about the needs of highly sensitive children. Provide a resource list in your manual so teachers have easy access to additional information they can refer to.

TIPS FOR EMPATH CHILDREN TO GET QUIET TIME IN SCHOOL

Many schools will go the extra mile to make allowances for highly sensitive children. But when it comes to things like quiet time, they may be unsure of how to work this into the hustle and bustle of a school day. You want to make your child's time at school as easy as possible, so give teachers some tips on how to implement quiet time into the day.

A Wooden Screen: Teachers can help reduce visual distractions by placing a wooden screen around a child's desk. It is a simple device that is placed on top of the desk. Some schools will have them, others won't; if not, you can purchase one yourself and leave it at the school.

Create a Quiet Space: This will depend on the setup of the classroom. If there is no space, maybe it can be made somewhere else in the school. Set up a small area with a chair, some cushions, books and headphones and an electronic device to play music. Your child can use this space when he/she needs quiet time to recharge. They can take five minutes out to read and listen to soothing music.

This quiet space can also be used for schoolwork. When there are different activities going on or the class is getting too loud and your child starts feeling overwhelmed, they can sit in their quiet space, put headphones on and work without being distracted by what's going on around them.

Noise-Reducing Headphones: It is inevitable that children are going to get loud, and you can't expect them to be quiet just because your child is highly sensitive. So once the teacher has provided instructions for work, let them put on a pair of noise-reducing headphones and get on with it.

Water Table or Sandpit: This works well for younger children when they start feeling overwhelmed. Place the table or sandpit outside the classroom so your child can get away from the high energy they would otherwise be surrounded by.

Run Errands: Perhaps the easiest way for a highly sensitive child to get quiet time during school is to have them run errands for the teacher. The above suggestions are great, but as mentioned at the start of this chapter, it is easy to single out highly sensitive children because of things like headphones and quiet areas. There is no doubt that the other children will make a big deal out of it even if they are told not to. To avoid this, the teacher can request that your child takes a trip to the principal's office or the library. If there is nothing to do, just let them go on a walk when temperatures start rising in the classroom.

STARTING SCHOOL FOR EMPATH CHILDREN

Now that you've chosen the right school to send your child to, the next step is overcoming the challenges of the first few days (in some cases weeks and months) of attendance. Going to school for the first time is difficult for children in general, but even more so for highly sensitive children. Your child might be different, so they may be excited about going to school and being in a new environment. But if you know your child is going to find it difficult, the advice in this section will give you a helping hand.

Why Children Get Distressed: As mentioned, small children in general have a difficult time on their first day of school. That's because changes in routines, people and environments outside the home can trigger an upsurge of the stress hormone cortisol. The brain is activated to believe there's a threat; in children, it causes clinginess, crying, sickness, tantrums, outbursts, sleeplessness and a poor appetite.

It's important to understand that their behavior is not because they are just being 'kids,' it's a biological reaction. They actually feel these things and it's essential that these feelings are validated. You can't explain biological reactions to preschool-aged children. But you can do so with older children and teenagers. Advise them that eating well, exercise, meditation and getting plenty of rest will help them with the transition.

For younger children, the main stressor is separation from the adult they have been totally dependent on for the first few years of their life. That person is usually their mother. Separation and change triggers the early warning system that is essential for our survival. Until the change becomes predictable and familiar, children will experience extreme anxiety about being in a different environment. The early warning response is even more severe for highly sensitive children. It is normal for this reaction to take place for a short period of time, but if it doesn't stop, it is referred to as separation distress. Some children can experience separation distress right up until their teenage years. However, if it continues for longer than three months, it is advised that you seek professional help for your child.

How to Reduce Stress For Young Children

When it comes to sending highly sensitive children to school for the first time, preparation is key. You will have heard (and may have even tried it yourself), that the best way to get your child used to preschool is to drop and dash. Experts believe this is a terrible idea in general, but it is even more so for highly sensitive children, and the consequences can be disastrous.

The most effective form of preparation is to get your child used to you not being there before they start school. The main aim is to get your child to trust you, and you can achieve this by telling them the truth; let them know you will be leaving them for a few hours throughout the day, but you will definitely be back. You can start developing this trust by playing hide and seek around the house. Here are some tips to limit the effects of separation distress:

- **Imaginary Protector:** One of the many positive characteristics about empath children is they've got vivid imaginations. Get your little one to imagine their ideal protector. What would he/she look like? What would their superpower be? These are just a few of the questions you can get your child to answer about their ideal protector. Get them to draw a picture of the protector and put it into their top pocket on the days they go to school.

- **Magic Kisses:** Before your child leaves the house, each parent should kiss one hand each. Those kisses are sealed and will stay there until he/she returns from school. You can also use a small clean jar to seal kisses; in the presence of your child, everyone in the house drops a kiss into the jar. The jar is sealed, and the kisses remain there forever. The jar is put at the bottom of your child's backpack, and knowing they've got kisses at the bottom of their bag from loved ones will help them feel secure when they get anxious.

- **Love Rainbows:** Play a game of love rainbows in the house, so one parent can be in the kitchen while your child is in the dining room, and you both send each other imaginary love rainbows from your hearts. During the school day, tell your child to send imaginary rainbows any time they miss you. They should imagine that you felt the love rainbow and sent one back to them.

- **Scented Toy:** Spray your perfume or Dad's aftershave onto a small toy and put it into their bag. Anytime your little one feels alone, they can take the toy out and hug it.

- **Funny Pictures:** Draw some funny pictures on paper, and let your child decide which one he/she finds the funniest. Draw that one onto their backpack, and anytime they start feeling anxious, they should look at it to make them laugh.

- **Pictures:** The safest place to put one is on a small bracelet around the wrist. Have a picture of Mom and Dad attached to the bracelet so they can look at it anytime they miss you. Some highly sensitive children will talk to the picture to comfort themselves even further.

- **Deep Breaths:** Most children of pre-school age are going to find breathing techniques difficult. But you can create a simple version that involves breathing out the butterflies. When they feel nervous and get the feeling of butterflies in their tummy, they should take three deep breaths to breathe out the butterflies hiding in their tummy.

- **Rub the Butterflies:** Teach your little one how to rub the butterflies in their tummy and tell them they are safe and will be okay until Mommy or Daddy gets back.

- **Singing:** Using your finger to draw circles in your child's hands while singing a song is a great comfort to them. Teach your child to do this to themselves when they start feeling overwhelmed. Touch and music encourage the release of 'feel-good' hormones.

- **Special Connection:** You will need to ask permission for this one, but in most cases, it should be fine once you've explained why. Help your child build a special connection with their teacher by having a framed picture of them in the home. Talk about the teacher with your little one, tell them how special the teacher is, how nice he/she is and that they should be really excited to be in their class.

WHY YOUR EMPATH CHILD DOESN'T LIKE THE GYM OR SWIMMING

If your child has an aversion to gym or swimming lessons, they will most likely have an emotional meltdown on those mornings. Parents of HSCs often don't understand why their children hate these classes so much. But it's important you understand why so you can let their teachers know why they struggle. It's essential for safety that your children know how to swim, so somehow, someway, they will need to get used to it (we will get into that later). But in the meantime, here are some common reasons why highly sensitive children don't like gym or swimming lessons:

The Noise: In a gym hall and swimming pool, the noise can be overwhelming because of the acoustic value in these rooms. They are large open spaces and sound vibrates off the walls, which makes noise sound louder than it is. That noise is exacerbated with the excitement of children as they splash about in the pool and run around in the gym.

Some highly sensitive children don't like noise because it causes a sensory overload which makes them feel uncomfortable. Even in normal settings, some HSCs hear noise louder than it actually is.

Tip: If you are lucky enough to have a pool at home, great! If not, take your child swimming during off-peak times and seasons when there are very few people in the pool. Furthermore, speak to different swimming schools to find out if there are any that cater to the needs of highly sensitive children.

Depending on how much your child can handle, you can also note gym and swimming lessons as bucket fillers and make sure the rest of the day is filled with very little activity.

Too Much Space: Empath children get overwhelmed when there is too much space with a lot of activity taking place. The changing rooms are usually quite small (even though this is an issue in itself), but once they come out, they are confronted with this huge space in which they have no control, and it scares them.

This is especially true in a gymnasium because there are so many activities taking place at once. Highly sensitive children like to know what they are going to do in advance; they like to imagine the activity. During phys ed time, students are not given this option.

Changing Rooms: Changing rooms are loud and crowded, and clothes are everywhere. This can be a sensory nightmare for empath children.

Tip: If there are individual cubicles, your child should get changed in one. Or, if your home is nearby, request that he/she is taken home to change. If the school is too far, and you've got the time, you can meet them at school when it's time for gym or swimming lessons and let them get changed in the car.

Smell: Chlorine is a very pungent smell, and gyms and locker rooms smell of sweaty bodies, stale feet and a host of other unpleasant odors. These smells can make HSCs feel very uncomfortable.

Tip: During swimming lessons, children are allowed to wear nose pegs to keep the water out. These can also act as a smell repellent. Additionally, give your child a rag doused in their favorite essential oils. They can smell it when they get back to the changing rooms.

Performance Anxiety: Many empath children are perfectionists and in school, swimming and gym lessons are monitored for performance. Their teachers will either give them on-the-spot feedback or approach students after the lesson. Empath children do not take constructive criticism well and feel as if they are being unfairly judged. Activities like swimming and running races can cause high levels of anxiety for HSCs because they are competing against other children. If they don't win, it is not uncommon for them to feel like a failure. Additionally, some HSCs find it difficult to accept encouragement; if a teacher tells them how well they are doing, they find it hard to believe.

Empath children feel very uncomfortable when they feel as if they are being observed. It triggers stress and anxiety, which makes swimming and gym lessons feel like an exam scenario in which failure is a possibility.

Tip: Some highly sensitive children are not emotionally ready to start such lessons. The best advice is to wait until the time is right.

Loud Voices: In lessons where children get excited and loud, and there is noise from splashing about in the water, or running around in the gym, teachers are forced to shout so the students can hear. There are also strict safety requirements the teachers must adhere to and they can come across as harsh when trying to enforce them. A gym teacher might see a dangerous situation about to unfold and be forced to shout to prevent it. A sudden loud voice can scare a highly sensitive child.

Overly Cautious: Empath children don't like taking risks so they will evaluate a situation for any potential danger before getting involved. That means it is very unlikely they will be jumping into a swimming pool on the count of three. Nor will they want to participate in any high-risk sports such as football. With that being said, there is no escaping the potential minefield at gyms and swimming pools. You've got balls being thrown around, six-foot-tall climbing frames, bats being swung and the deep end in the swimming pool. If an HSC stops to think about it, there are so many opportunities for them to get hurt, they'd rather not participate and risk getting injured.

Tip: Arrange a meeting with the gym and swimming instructor and let them know how difficult it is for your child to take part in such activities. The hope is that the teacher is understanding enough so your child trusts they are in good hands during those lessons.

Finally: It's important that you don't give up, because once highly sensitive children become familiar with their environment and they know what to expect, they are less likely to panic.

Tips to Handle Going Back to School With Empath Children

As mentioned, empath children don't like change, and as much as they don't like being in their current school environment, sometimes the devil you know is better than the devil you don't. The thought of changing schools and being around new children and teachers might scare them. Therefore, you will need to break the news of change to them gently.

Highly sensitive children enjoy the security of their home. And after a long summer vacation where they have got used to a certain routine and schedule, breaking that to go back to school will come with some challenges because they don't adjust to change as quickly as other children. However, if you put a plan in place a few weeks before they are due to go back to school, everything will work out the way it's supposed to.

Invite Friends Around: If your child is just starting a new school, find out who some of the students will be in his/her class and invite them over one at a time for a play date. Even if they are going back to the same school and you can invite the friends they already have, you can also find out if there will be any new students and do the same.

Regular play dates will help strengthen the relationships your child already has and develop new ones if they need to before the term starts. Your child will feel a lot more comfortable going back to school once they get used to seeing new or familiar faces on a regular basis.

Get in the Classroom: Contact the school principal and arrange a time that you and your child can come and visit the new classroom. Getting familiar with their environment will eliminate some of the anxiety associated with spending time in a place they are not used to. Do this a couple of weeks before school starts, which shouldn't be a problem if the school is sympathetic to the needs of empath children.

In most cases, your child will have a different teacher at the start of the school year. It will help to get your child acquainted with the teacher a few minutes before the start of class, as this will not only give your son/daughter the chance to get to know their teacher, it will also give you the opportunity to give them some information about your child. To make sure they don't forget, you might want to type out a few bullet points summarizing your manual.

Time for Bed: During school holidays, it is the norm to allow children to go to bed later than normal, and to sleep in. A week or two before school, start getting them back into the routine of going to bed early and waking up early. This will give their bodies the chance to get used to their new schedule once they get back to school.

Start Practicing: How does your child get to school? Do they walk, do you drive them there or does someone pick them up? However your child gets to school, make that journey with them. Make things clear, such as where you will pick them up, where they will line up, where they will get off the bus etc.

Preparation: The night before school, make sure everything is done; their bags are packed, school clothes ready, and lunches made. If your child is sensitive to touch and they are wearing new clothes, make sure they try them on before the first day of school, so if there is any problem with comfort, you can make alterations or change the outfit. Preparation is essential to your child being calm and present in the morning before school because if they feel rushed, it will send them into a meltdown.

Additionally, you want to go over the structure of the day: what time they will wake up, have a shower, have breakfast, how they are getting to and from school and so on. Encourage your child to talk about any fears they might have and validate them if they do.

WHEN EMPATH CHILDREN FEEL OUT OF PLACE

I have said this several times throughout the book, and I will say it again. Empath children do not have a disorder or disability, and nor are they mentally challenged. They are just different and there is nothing wrong with that. However, not only will your child sense they are different, but other children will point it out, and sometimes they can be quite mean about it. Most children will try and fit in with their peer group, but oftentimes, they won't feel comfortable. It is challenging to find a balance between being yourself and not standing out, so this can make highly sensitive children feel bad. There are a lot of benefits to being highly sensitive, but there are also some negative aspects that you can't ignore.

You will find that as young as preschool age, if another child is upset because they miss their mom, your child will also feel upset. If a child scrapes their knee, your child will feel their pain and spend the rest of the day and night worrying about the child who fell. At a certain age, your son or daughter will realize that no one else in their class is crying because another kid banged their head. If you have other children who are not highly sensitive, your child will start to notice they are different from their sibling(s) too.

Empath children need time to unwind; unlike other children, they can't come home from school, change their clothes and go straight out to play. They need to process their day, get used to the transition and allow their body to adjust. After a while, they will start asking why their friends don't need time to adjust before going out to play after school.

As much as children like attention, they don't want to stand out, and when they notice this is the case, they will start asking why. As they grow older, this becomes increasingly important to them. Unfortunately, we live in a world where it's not okay to be different; fashionable means you've got to wear a certain style of clothes, attractive means you've got to look a certain way; and success means you've got to live a certain lifestyle. The majority of people in the world don't fit into that box, and many people spend their lives trying to conform to an unattainable standard. Accepting who you are is a skill you've got to master, and it's essential that parents teach their highly sensitive children to accept and love who they are. If people do learn this skill, they do so later on in life after having experienced many hardships from trying so hard to be like everyone else. The good news is that you can teach your child this skill from a young age so they don't grow up feeling out of place.

Be Available: Empath children are made to feel different because of how other people (both children and adults) react to their behavior. One of the main consequences of this treatment is withdrawal: the HSC will stop sharing their observations and thoughts with others because they don't want to be judged.

Become a safe haven for your child and let them know they can speak to you about anything, whether it's the way they feel, something they've noticed, that someone reacted towards them in a way they didn't like, or that they even suspected a spiteful reaction from someone. Some highly sensitive children will keep their thoughts to themselves until they get home, where they know people are not going to judge them for what they've got to say.

Empath children are often very wise and insightful for their age, and it is not uncommon for their peers not to understand them. When they are raised in a safe and nurturing space, and they are taught that who they are is a valuable gift to the world, HSCs will feel more confident sharing their thoughts and opinions outside the home.

Teach Them to Understand Who They Are: As you know, empath children pick up other people's emotions. If a teacher is not in the best of moods, an HSC will sense this and the lesson won't go as well for them, or they'll become concerned for the teacher. For a child, carrying the burden of other people's emotions is tiring and confusing,

It's essential that empath children learn to tell the difference between their emotions and the emotions of other people they are carrying, and when it's enough just to listen to someone's issues without feeling the need to solve the problem. Every highly sensitive child must develop the skill of freeing themselves of emotions, so they are not overloaded with feelings that don't belong to them. Here are some tips on how to do this:

- **Label Their Feelings:** You will know when your child is feeling someone else's heavy emotions because their behavior will change. This change will be particularly apparent if you have been with them all day and nothing out of the ordinary has taken place. Therefore, the first step is to help your child label how they are feeling; this will allow them to gain some distance from the emotions.

- **Whose Emotions Are They?** To determine whose emotions your child is feeling, you will need to ask them some gentle questions. Empath children pick up emotions from things they've watched, heard or personally experienced. Ask questions like:
  - Did you watch something on TV that upset you?
  - Did you hear something on the radio that upset you?
  - Did you hear Mommy or Daddy say something that upset you?
  - Did someone say something to you to upset you?
  - Did you think about something that made you sad?

It is difficult for a child to separate their emotions from someone else's, but with time this will become easier for them.

Raise Awareness: The moment you realize your child is feeling emotions that don't belong to them, encourage your son/daughter to raise their awareness of what's happening. Teaching your child to say the word 'compassion' will give them a way of being intentional about focusing on what they can do to be supportive instead of allowing the emotion to overwhelm them.

Body Awareness: This step will depend on your child's age and level of maturity. Get them to take a deep breath and pay attention to the location in their body where they feel the most neutral, grounded or calm. It might be their finger, toe or stomach; get them to focus their attention on that area and use it as a centering force so they can remain grounded while they process and release the feelings they have taken on. When one place of the body is calm, it will help create some balance when the rest of the body is overwhelmed.

Send the Emotions Back: Teach your child that it is not their responsibility to take on other people's burdens or emotions. Your child may justify this weight they are carrying by thinking they are helping the other person. But in most cases (especially when the person whose emotions they are carrying is not present), that individual is not even aware that their feelings have been absorbed by someone who has such compassion for them. The reality is that they are not helping anyone, but they are harming themselves. To send the emotions back, they can say something like, *"I am releasing the emotional pain that doesn't belong to me back to the person it came from."* Remind your child that they don't need to feel guilty about this because people can't grow if they don't process their own emotions.

Visualization to Release Emotions: Again, this step will depend on the age and maturity of your child, but as a final step, it helps to get them to fully release the emotions they are carrying. Encourage your child further by doing it *with* them. Get your son or daughter to sit for a few seconds with their eyes closed and imagine water running through their body and washing off anything negative that doesn't belong there. You can make the visualization session more effective by playing soft sounds of running water in the background.

HOME SCHOOLING

Parents in general are becoming so dissatisfied with public school education that they are looking for other options. As the parent of an empath child, you may be unable to find a school in your local area willing to cater to their needs. So what do you do? The choices are limited; it's either send them to school or home school them. The question is: which one is going to be most beneficial to your child's education and emotional well-being?

According to the National Home Education Research Institute, an estimated 2 million children are home schooled in the United States every year. There are both advantages and disadvantages to home schooling.

Advantage 1 – Your Child Feels Safe: Empath children will never feel one hundred percent safe when going to school. There is always going to be an element of fear because their days are unpredictable. They don't know when things are going to get chaotic and loud, and they don't know if the teacher they have gotten used to is going to be off sick. They don't know if there is going to be a fire drill, and there are many other unpredictable events that could take place throughout the day. As a parent, you have complete control over what goes on in your home.

Advantage 2 – You Know How to Handle Your Child: Over time, you will get to learn the things that trigger your child. Random things like the flicker of lights, loud classmates or uncomfortable clothes can cause hyper-reactivity and overwhelm which make it difficult for empath children to concentrate. At home, children don't need to wear shoes and they can wear comfortable clothes. They can work with the dog sitting on their lap, have soothing music playing in the background or work in silence. You know what works best for your child, and you can switch things up as and when you need to in order to help your son or daughter reach their learning goals.

Advantage 3 – Children Learn More: Empath children need to learn at their own pace; with all the shuffling between classes, roll call and other random events that take place throughout the school day, it's difficult for your child to focus. Additionally, when home schooling, your son or daughter can spend more time focusing on their own passions instead of following a rigid curriculum that doesn't appeal to them.

Advantage 4 – Outdoor Playtime: One of the most common punishments in schools is to make children stand along the fence during playtime. As you will have experienced, empath children are often disciplined because teachers don't understand their unique traits and confuse them for bad behavior. The combination of being punished and not being able to play outside and release pent up energy is a recipe for disaster for an empath child and can cause severe emotional overwhelm. Spending time outside, whether it's to bounce on a trampoline, or just sit in nature is extremely beneficial for empath children. It centers them so they can regain focus and get back to work.

Advantage 5 – No Need for Explanations: Sending your child to school means that at least once a year (sometimes several times a year), you are going to need to have a meeting with your child's teacher and explain the complexities of an empath's personality traits. The reality is that although the majority of teachers want the best for your child, having to rearrange things because they have an empath child in the class simply adds to their workload. More often than not, most of what you say to them will go in one ear and out the other. And you can be pretty sure the majority of them are not going to take time out of their busy schedules to study the manual you created.

Disadvantage 1 – Can You Afford it? Can you afford a drop in income to teach your child at home? In most cases the mother becomes the teacher and has to give up work to do so.

Disadvantage 2 – It is Time Consuming: Home schooling is not a couple of hours a day; the schedule is the same as if your child was in a regular school. As well as teaching skills, you will also need good bookkeeping and time management skills. Any of these jobs individually is difficult, but when you are doing all three it can be very challenging.

Disadvantage 3 – It is Challenging: Teaching may be the most challenging aspect of the job. Although you graduated high school many years ago, unless you continued in one of the subjects as a career, you will have forgotten the majority of what you were taught. So basically you are going to have to go back to school, not literally, but to teach yourself so that you can teach your child. Fortunately there are a wide range of online resources that will be able to assist you with this process.

Finally: Whatever you decide, you will need to think carefully about your decision. Remember your child's education is at stake here. You don't want to start home schooling your child and then realize that you have taken on too much of a responsibility and must send them back to school. Weigh your options up carefully, and plan for years ahead instead of just a few months down the line.

Home schooling is like a full-time job. Is that a responsibility you are willing to take on for a good few years?

Home schooling logistics can become suffocating if you are not familiar with them. Educating your child at home should be an exciting and invigorating experience for both of you. So don't allow the complexity of the information to overwhelm you. Here is some helpful insight to assist you in understanding the basics of home schooling.

DECIDING TO HOME SCHOOL

There are a multitude of factors you will need to consider when looking at home schooling; each person will have different requirements depending on family needs. Communicate with other families who home school by contacting them online or visiting them in person. Find out if there is a home school support group in your area and ask whether they provide information or events for families that are considering home schooling. Some groups will connect you to a mentor or host a question-and-answer evening that you can attend.

HOME SCHOOLING AND THE LAW

Every state has their own laws concerning home schooling. It is imperative that you find out what they are. Home schooling is legal in all states, however some states have stricter regulations than others. The age of your child and whether or not they have already enrolled in public school could have an effect on whether you will be able to legally home school your child.

Start How You Intend to Finish

Once you are certain that you are going to home school, you will need to remain positive and focused about your decision. The transition period is going to be difficult, especially if your child does not want to home school. You will need to allow time for everyone to adjust to this new way of learning.

Listen to your instincts in regard to home schooling your children and take advice from parents who have been home schooling for a while.

A Support Group

Meet regularly with other parents who home school their children. This can be a challenge in itself, as you need to find the right family that connects with yours. Since your child is not going to be in school, it is also important that they have home school friends, so they don't feel alienated.

The Right Curriculum

It can be a difficult task to choose the right curriculum for home-schooling. There are so many choices that it is easy to spend more money than expected and still not find the right curriculum for your child. Depending on the state, you may not need to purchase a curriculum immediately. You can print a free online curriculum as well as use your local library for assistance.

UNDERSTANDING RECORD KEEPING

It is essential that you are efficient with record keeping during your child's home school years. Your records can be as simple as a handwriting notepad, or you can use one of the many sophisticated computer programs. Your state may require that you write a progress report while you are home schooling your child.

Even if your state doesn't require you to produce home school reports, you should make a habit of doing them anyway for your own records and so you can monitor your child's progress.

SCHEDULING

Home schoolers typically have a lot of freedom when it comes to creating a schedule. However, it can take some time to find out what works best for the family. What's important is that once you have decided on a schedule, you stick to it. Here are some points to consider:

- Your partner's work schedule
- When do your children work best?
- What other commitments do you have within or outside the home?

HOME SCHOOL METHODS

There are several home school methods you can use. You may have to go through a period of trial and error, but make sure you invest some time in finding what is right for your child. Don't feel disheartened if you try out one or even a few methods and they don't work for you; this is normal. You may want to mix and match some of the methods. For example, you might want to try a combination of unit study techniques, the Charlotte Mason method, and unschooling.

The most important thing is to remain open about home schooling methods because it's an important decision to make.

This basic information will help you begin your home schooling journey. It is not going to be an easy decision because as you can see, there is a lot to consider. However, with careful planning and determination this could be one of the best decisions you make for your child.

CHAPTER 12:

FRIENDSHIPS AND PLAYDATES WITH EMPATH CHILDREN

Whether your child is an introvert or an extrovert, empath children have a hard time making friends at school. In general, people just don't 'get' them. Empaths are unique in their own right and it takes a special kind of person to really get to know an empath for who they are instead of focusing on their differences.

It is not uncommon for empath children to appear wiser than their years; in most cases, they prefer hanging around their parents to socializing with their peer groups. They would rather stay at home and play alone then go to Jonny's birthday party.

WHY EMPATH CHILDREN FIND IT DIFFICULT TO MAKE FRIENDS

Children need a good set of friends because it is beneficial for their emotional and social development, as well as their self-confidence. It's not that empath children don't like playing and having fun like other children; they are also eager to make friends. The problem is they don't like walking into situations they are unfamiliar with. Empath children would rather stand back and observe from a distance to see if it's something they can handle before jumping in. Some children can be a bit rough, and empaths don't like aggression. In most cases, kids are just being kids, but due to the highly sensitive nature of the empath child, things like rolling around in the sand are not the slightest bit appealing to them. Furthermore, crowds, noise, smells and other factors can cause overstimulation.

If you've got empath boys, you may find that they prefer female friends. Empath boys would rather play with girls because they enjoy gentle play and are less likely to engage in competitive behavior. Parents tend to get worried when they notice this and fear that the child might become effeminate. But it's nothing to be concerned about. They are just more comfortable around girls and you should nurture their interactions instead of discouraging them or you will find that your child will start self-isolating.

SEE THINGS FROM THEIR PERSPECTIVE

Imagine getting invited to a party, and when you get there, and you don't know anyone. Everyone's in their own little world having their own conversations. You are introduced to a few people, but they unintentionally make you feel like the odd one out. Basically, you are not one of the 'cool kids' so they pretty much ignore you. How would you feel? Not good, right? And then to make matters worse, the friend who invited you begins forcing you to interact with everyone, but you've only been in the room for five minutes.

Most people don't walk into an unfamiliar environment and jump into conversations with people. They will stand back and observe the social dynamics before they start mingling. In some cases, no matter how polite or extroverted you are, you would rather stay alone in a corner because those there are just not your type of people. Do you not find it aggravating when you are pushed to do things that don't appeal to you?

When you force your child to play with children they are not comfortable with, it's exactly the same. As an adult, you can fake it, or simply get in your car and drive off, while children have neither the emotional capability to fake it, nor the independence to remove themselves from a situation if they don't like it. Instead, they react by yelling, hitting, crying, having a tantrum, or internalizing how they feel and shutting down. So, the next question is: how can we resolve this?

LEAD BY EXAMPLE

Parents have a bad habit of enforcing change in their children without looking within first. Children in general are like sponges who absorb everything in their environments. Due to the highly sensitive nature of empath children, they pick up on every last detail. All parents want their children to make friends and be happy and healthy. When parents of empath children notice that they spend a lot of time alone, they worry, get anxious and do things like force their little ones to make friends with children that make them uncomfortable. Despite how frustrating this might be for you, it will help to remember that it's even more frustrating for your child. But the more patient and understanding you are with them, the better things will be for everyone.

You are your child's role model so they are going to look to you for guidance in terms of how to act and react. Therefore, it's important that you do your best not to express how you really feel when you are around them. Instead, be as empathetic and patient as you can. Hiding your feelings is not an easy task when it hurts to see your child struggle, but getting emotional about it will only make the situation worse.

When you go out and there are other children around but your child is hanging onto your skirt complaining about the mess, the smell and the noise, saying things like, "You need to go and play with the other children," is the worst thing you can say. I have seen it myself several times. When a parent doesn't understand that their child is an empath, they get very frustrated and do things like shout in a low-pitched voice in the child's face while squeezing both arms and semi-shaking them. Not a good move! These public displays of aggression can be disastrous for empath children. Instead, do the following:

Empathize: Empath children need to feel that their parents understand them. They feel secure when they are encouraged to express how they really feel. Listen as they tell you why they are uncomfortable at the birthday party. Let your little one know that it's okay for them to feel this way.

Validate Their Feelings: It's easy for parents to launch into lecture mode when their kids start acting up. But lecturing doesn't work for empath children because when they start feeling overwhelmed, they want someone to listen to them and validate how they feel. At this point, help your child label their feelings by saying things like, "I can see that the noise in this park is frustrating you," or "I can sense that Michael's wrestling matches are uncomfortable for you." When an empath child can label their feelings, they find it easier to overcome them and move on.

Acceptance: When your son or daughter grabs hold of your leg and won't leave you alone at a family gathering, let them. Pick them up, give them a hug and allow them to stay with you. When you push your child away, it signals that their behavior is annoying you and they are not accepted. When you empathize and validate their feelings, it soothes their anxiety, knowing they have a safe haven in you.

HELP YOUR CHILD BUILD FRIENDSHIPS

It's important to allow your child to go out and make their own friends. But empaths need additional guidance and support when it comes to socializing with their peers. Here are a few tips on how you can help your child build friendships:

Develop Their Social Skills: Empath children have a tendency to isolate themselves as a defense mechanism that helps them deal with being highly sensitive. This is a delicate balance, but it's important that you don't allow this to become the norm. As mentioned earlier, forcing your child to make friends is a bad idea, but teaching them about good social behavior can help. Good social skills allow children to have satisfying and healthy peer relationships now and in the future. As your little one gets older, their social skills will need refining. Children are not born with social skills; they learn them, and parents are their teachers. Throughout the day, look for opportunities to help your child improve their social skills. Focus on things like the importance of taking turns, sharing and losing gracefully. Model the behavior you want to see in your children. Remember, empaths are extremely sensitive to their environment and they will internalize everything you do. Here are some tips on how you can help improve your child's social skills:

- **Lead with Their Interests:** Children are always going to feel more comfortable when they are doing the things they enjoy. Whether it's playing a musical instrument or playing a sport or game, getting them involved in their favorite activities helps develop social skills because it gives your child the opportunity to meet like-minded individuals that they will feel more comfortable socializing with. It is also important that your little one learns to associate with people that have different interests, but leading with *their* interests is a good place to start and you can build from here.

- **Encourage Them to Ask Questions:** Empath children get nervous when a conversation doesn't flow. It makes them anxious, and they assume the person has no interest in speaking to them. Disinterest is rarely the issue, as it's natural for conversations to slow down and for both parties to run out of things to say. Among emotionally intelligent adults, or good conversationalists, there's an understanding that this is a good time to ask questions because it helps push the conversation forward. Teach your child that the best way to get to know someone is to ask questions. You can get them involved by having them write down a list of questions and then taking part in a role-playing session with them.

- **Picture Cards:** Kids will be kids, and they have very little emotional intelligence. Everyone speaks through their emotions, and children are particularly good at this, but most children don't pick up on it because it's a skill they've yet to learn. You can give your child a head start in understanding social cues by using picture cards. They can help interpret visual cues such as frustration, sadness, boredom, anger and happiness. You can take this a step further by using video clips in which different emotions are acted out.

- **Practice Sharing:** Empath children get very attached to their toys and they don't like sharing. The strong attachment they have to their toys often leads to tears and meltdowns during social gatherings. Selfishness is not an admirable quality. The practice of sharing is something you can engage in daily. Taking turns to go first and last can take place at the dinner table, getting in and out of the car, etc.

- **Know Their Limits:** Some empath children are going to be more sociable than others. It is your job as a parent to know their limits because you don't want to end up scaring them. Learn your child's strengths and encourage him/her in that area. It is also important to encourage them in their areas of weakness, but make sure you are not forcing them to do anything they are not comfortable with.

Role Plays and Scripts: Empath children don't like surprises; they prefer being in control and knowing what's going to happen next. If you are going somewhere that involves socializing, role play so your child knows what to expect. Talk about the questions people are likely to ask and how they plan on responding. Engage in a role-playing scenario with the questions and answers as this will help your child feel more confident when the time comes.

Teach Them About Real Friendships: Empaths are often taken advantage of because they find it difficult to speak up for themselves. Unfortunately, the mean kids usually have a field day with empath children because they take their kindness as a weakness. Teach your child what it means to have good friends; that they are people who don't make them feel bad, will compromise, and encourage them when they feel down, and that true friends accept each other for who they are and take each other's feelings into consideration.

Partner with Your Child: Become your child's number one advocate. Let them know you are rooting for them, and that you will walk with them every step of the way. Your little one is going to need direction and assistance when it comes to making friends, but confidence and self-esteem starts in the home. The positive impact you have on your child will determine how well they cope in social situations.

What is a Play Date?

Empath children struggle with anxiety, especially when in a group setting. To cope with this, they will often go off and play on their own, which can make them appear 'weird' and 'anti-social' to other children.

When children get together in groups, they will typically conform to the norms and the standards of that group, and if the leader decides that Sally is a misfit and no one should play with her, then that's exactly what will happen. On the other hand, when kids have one-on-one time together, their interactions are different. There are no other children to impress and they can focus on getting to know each other a bit better. The idea is that if your child can develop a few friendships outside of a group setting by having individual play dates, he/she will find it easier to fit in during classroom sessions. The younger you start your little one off having play dates, the easier socializing will become as they grow up. It will be a little awkward for the both of you at the start, but once you get used to it, you'll be fine. Here are some tips on how to have a successful play date:

Speak to the Teachers: As important as it is for empath children to make friends, they can't socialize with everyone. This is where it gets tricky because it's essential that you find like-minded children, or your first play date will be a complete disaster. If your son or daughter is sensitive to noise, inviting the loudest kid in the class over for a play date isn't going to work out too well. If your child is sensitive to touch, a touchy feely type child won't be a good idea either. Your best bet is to start by speaking to the teachers. Since they will already have an understanding of your child's needs, and they are familiar with the personalities of the children in the classroom, they will know who will be best suited as a friend for your empath child.

Make Contact with Parents: This is probably the most awkward part when it comes to play dates. To begin, you will need to make contact with the parents of children in your child's class. Brace yourself because it won't be easy; most people have zero understanding about empaths, and some people might be a bit intimidated by it. But most parents will be very understanding, empathetic and cooperative. In terms of making contact, schools typically have email lists of parents, and I have found that this is the most effective way of communicating your requests. In this way, if they are willing to go ahead, the parents will offer their phone number and you can arrange a telephone conversation to explain things further and make the necessary arrangements.

Have the Play Dates at Home: Empath children are more comfortable at home than anywhere else. By hosting the play date at home, you can ensure your child is in a familiar environment where they can relax and be themselves. He/she is less likely to get overwhelmed and anxious, and if they do, you will be there. You can control the environment in your home by eliminating anything that causes your child to feel stressed out. Once they get used to having play dates at home, you can slowly start introducing them outside the home.

Plan Your Activities: Empath children like order and structure, so they are most confident when they know what to expect in a situation. Most children can get on with it and find ways to entertain themselves; for some empath children, this can be overwhelming. Additionally, empath children don't like being in the spotlight. When parents arrange the games for the play date, it puts the attention on the activity, and takes it off the child. You can of course get your son or daughter involved in the activity planning process, as long as it is done before the guest arrives, so they don't feel under pressure. If your child is protective of their favorite toys and they don't like sharing them, don't involve those toys in the game or you will end up dealing with a meltdown situation.

Play Date Activity Ideas: All empath children are different; you will probably need to experiment with a few ideas before you find what works. In general, the following have been pretty successful:

- **Team Player Games:** Even though these are team games, be sure to remove the competitive elements because it could cause your child to become overwhelmed. Some good team player games include hide and seek, balloon toss and spy board games.
- **Building Forts:** Work together and create something fun.
- **Legos/Sand Table:** A great way to have lots of interaction and share toys.

GAMES TO PLAY WITH EMPATH CHILDREN

- Watercolor painting, paint the deck, fences etc.
- Arts and crafts from recycled materials
- Non-competitive board games
- Hide and seek

- Sculptures out of toothpicks and marshmallows
- Lemonade stand
- Play-doh
- Paper airplanes
- Exploring sensory bins, water beads, noodles, beans
- Balloons
- Making slime
- Carboard box games
- Tie dye
- Bubbles
- Science experiments
- Dress ups – princesses/superheroes etc
- Sidewalk chalk
- Play tea party/restaurant
- Fort-making using tables, chairs, blankets etc
- Rock painting
- Sandbox/sand table
- Legos
- Nature scavenger hunt
- Baking – brownies, cupcakes, muffins, cookies

FILMS TO WATCH WITH HIGHLY SENSITIVE CHILDREN

- *Winnie the Pooh*
- *Sing*
- *The Secret Life of Pets*
- *Ratatouille*
- *The Peanuts Movie*
- *Minions*
- *Mary Poppins*
- Disney nature movies

- *Despicable Me*
- *Curious George*
- *The Aristocats*
- *101 Dalmatians*

Allow your child to take charge and pay attention to how things are going. If he/she seems comfortable engaging in some unstructured play, go ahead and switch things up. If it looks like they need some help, don't be afraid to jump in.

Short and Sweet: How long your play dates last will depend on your child's capabilities. But in general, the shorter the better; between 45 minutes and 2 hours is usually the sweet spot. Even if the play date is going well, don't extend it, because when empath children get tired, they get overwhelmed.

After-Play Discussion: You can make improvements on play dates by having a discussion with your child afterwards about how they think it went. You can talk about it over dinner or before bed. During this time, celebrate any successes, no matter how small. If they feel the need, let your child write or draw about the experience in their journal. This will help them determine which parts of the play date they weren't comfortable with, and the parts they enjoyed.

Keep it Up: Even if you or your child don't think the play date went well, try again. It may have been the wrong friend, the wrong games, or just one of those days. Eventually, you will find what works for you and you can stick with that.

CONCLUSION

Many empath children are a goldmine of vast, untapped potential, and because they are raised in the wrong environments, they don't flourish. Others, like myself, were treated with such contempt that our value was stomped out of us.

We live in a world filled with so much depravity; just turn on the TV, listen to the radio or open a newspaper and all you see is destruction. Wars, abuse, corruption, addiction, depression and much more. Empaths are the much-needed light in this dark world; they have an inner calling to be saviors that is programmed deep into their psyches.

The world needs sensitive, selfless people who have a deep desire to bring out the best in everyone around them. If there were more empaths in the world, it would be a much better place, so I really feel it's essential to give them a solid foundation to build on. Many of the world's most compassionate people were highly sensitive. Due to your child's naturally intuitive nature, he/she knows they are different. And they will feel out of place because of it. You can help reduce those feelings of isolation by telling them about the many highly sensitive people who changed the world. It will encourage them to remember these people when times get tough:

Mother Teresa: Mother Teresa lived her life fully devoted to the poor and the sick. She felt deep empathy for the suffering and expressed her devotion by choosing to live among them. She opened leper houses, orphanages and hospices all over India. By 2012, her organization, Missionaries of Charity, had been established in 133 countries. Mother Teresa gave many people hope during their dying moments. She won numerous awards for her service to humanity, including the Nobel Peace Prize, the Templeton Prize and the Golden Honor of the Nation.

Martin Luther King: Martin Luther King, Jr. had so much empathy for African American people that he spent his entire life fighting for equality. He was a pastor, activist, and director the of the Civil Rights Movement. King is renowned for his non-violent approach to justice based on his Christian beliefs. His famous 'I Have a Dream' speech, given in Washington D.C in 1963 is still quoted today. He was awarded the Nobel Peace Prize, the Spingarn Medal, the Congressional Gold Medal and many more.

Albert Einstein: Highly sensitive people are completely in tune with their instincts and are fully aware when their inner man is speaking to them. In the early 1920s, Einstein developed the theory of general relativity. The entire scientific community disagreed with it, and he was met with fierce opposition. However, he refused to back down and insisted that his work was credible. Today, Einstein's general theory of relativity is known as one of the most remarkable scientific achievements.

Mahatma Gandhi: Gandhi was so sensitive as a child that he was overly nervous and shy. He had a terrible fear of public speaking, despite the fact that he regularly spoke to crowds of thousands of people. Gandhi embraced his unique gift and became a fearless warrior who saved his people from British rule and fought against racial oppression in South Africa. Today, he is known as one of the most powerful leaders in history.

Eleanor Roosevelt: Eleanor Roosevelt was the wife of United States president Franklin D. Roosevelt. She took advantage of her position and used it for social activism. Roosevelt advocated against racial inequality and for women's rights. During the First World War, she volunteered with the Red Cross, providing disaster relief and serving meals to soldiers traveling through Washington's Union station. In 1927, Roosevelt played a role in establishing the Val-Kill Industries. These were just a few of Eleanor Roosevelt's achievements during her lifetime.

Nicole Kidman: Nicole Kidman is an Australian actress who has starred in many films including *Eyes Wide Shut*, *Moulin Rouge* and *The Others*. Kidman is also known for her role as a humanitarian; she raised half a million dollars for a woman's cancer charity and is a champion for female voices in the male-dominated Hollywood Industry. She continuously supports women's causes and has won several awards including Australia's highest civilian honor. Kidman believes saving lives and solving problems is much more important and rewarding than her career as an actress.

Ed Sheeran: Popstar Ed Sheeran is very open about his empath nature. He wears his heart on his sleeve and expresses his emotions through his music. A lot of his songs are often used for the first dance at weddings, which indicates that he is deeply in tune with the inner feelings of his core audience. Sheeran is also exceptionally humble; he does not define himself by his wealth and is notorious for wearing the same clothes he wore before he became famous.

Larry King: As a television presenter, Larry King is an extrovert who enjoys being in the limelight. But at the same time, he is capable of developing deep connections with his interviewees because he listens intently, he is extremely compassionate, and people trust him enough to confide in him, which is one of the main characteristics of an empath.

Mel Gibson: He is one of the most famous actors and directors in Hollywood. His highly sensitive nature enables him to play and direct impassioned roles that have a profound effect on his audience. He has earned numerous awards throughout the years for his outstanding performances.

I believe that empaths are among the most powerful people on the planet. As a parent of an empath child, I empathize with how frustrating it can become when you don't know what it's like to walk in their shoes and have a limited understanding of what they are going through. Even though it's hard work, don't give up! By diligently applying the principles laid out in this book, life will eventually become a lot easier for you. Once empaths develop self-acceptance and self-love, stop resisting their gift and learn to work with their sensitivity, they thrive in any environment. I've seen it happen over and over again. When they start following their passions, living from their heart, and tapping into the inner wisdom of their spirit, something magical happens.

And finally, look after yourself! Raising an empath child is fulfilling, rewarding and exhausting. As you've read, there are so many additional measures you've got to put in place. For instance, you can't just put your child in front of the TV when you need to fold the laundry. You can't just allow your child to go swimming with his/her friends. Everything has to be planned and monitored, which can cause you additional stress. Be sure to take time out to relax and recharge your batteries; a stressed-out parent is no use to an empath child. They need you to be fully alert and aware at all times.

My prayer is that after reading this book, you are now equipped to train your children to become the fearless empath warriors they were created to be.

I wish you every success on your journey as a parent raising an empath child!

THANKS FOR READING!

I really hope you enjoyed this book, and most of all got more value from it than you had to give.

It would mean a lot to me if you left an Amazon review – I will reply to all questions asked!

Simply find this book on Amazon, scroll to the reviews section, and click "Write a customer review".

Or Scan the QR Code on Your Phone:

Be sure to check out my email list, where I am constantly adding tons of value. The best way to get on the list currently is by visiting www.pristinepublish.com/empathbonus and entering your email.

Here I'll provide actionable information that aims to improve your enjoyment of life. I'll update you on my latest books, and I'll even send free e-books that I think you'll find useful.

Kindest regards,

ALSO BY
Judy Dyer

Grasp a better understanding of your gift and how you can embrace every part of it so your life is enriched day by day.

Visit: www.pristinepublish.com/judy

Or Scan the QR Code on Your Phone:

REFERENCES

Acevedo, B; *The Highly Sensitive Brain: Research, Assessment, and Treatment of Sensory Processing Sensitivity* (1st ed.); Academic Press; 2020.

ADAA; 2020; *Treatment.*

Aron, E; *The Highly Sensitive Child: Helping Our Children Thrive When The World Overwhelms Them*; Harmony; 2002.

Bartoshuk, L; 2019; *Speaking of Psychology: Why We Like the Foods We Like;* APA.

Bell, L; 2015; *Connection Between Anorexia and Anxiety Disorders;* Eating Disorder Hope.

Children's Bureau; 2018; *Why The First 5 Years of Child Development Are So Important.*

Common Sense Media; 2021; *Reviews For What Your Kids Want to Watch (Before They Watch It).*

Crawford, C; *The Highly Intuitive Child: A Guide to Understanding and Parenting Unusually Sensitive and Empathic Children*; Hunter House; 2009.

Grow; 2021; *How Much Sleep Do Children Need?*

Gruber, S; 2019; *Mis-attunement: The Invisible ACE;* ACEs Connection.

IGI Global; 2021; *What is Reflective Thinking?*

Knuppel, A; Shipley, M.J.; Llewellyn C.H & Brunner, E.J; 2017; *Sugar Intake From Sweet Food and Beverages;* US National Library of Medicine.

Kurcinka, M. S; *Raising Your Spirited Child, Third Edition: A Guide for Parents Whose Child Is More Intense, Sensitive, Perceptive, Persistent, and Energetic* (3rd ed.); William Morrow Paperbacks; 2015.

Lyons, C., & Welsh, J. *Being an Empath Kid* (Illustrated ed.); White Light Publishing House; 2014

Md, O. J. *The Empath's Survival Guide: Life Strategies for Sensitive People* (Reprint ed.). Sounds True; 2018

Meighan, F; *The Empathic Parent's Guide to Raising a Highly Sensitive Child: Parenting Strategies I Learned to Understand and Nurture My Child's Gift;* Independently Published; 2020.

Mennillo, M; 2019; *What is Co-Regulation?;* OTFC.

Morin, A; 2021; *5 Problems Kids With Overprotective Parents Are Likely to Experience in Adulthood, According to Science;* Inc.

Pantazi, J; 2019; *8 Negative Effects of Overprotective Parenting;* Youniverse.

Seligman , L & Ollendick, T.H.; 2012; *Cognitive Behavioral Therapy For Anxiety Disorders in Youth;* US National Library of Medicine.

Taylor, J.M.; 2016; *Mirror Neurons After a Quarter Century: New Light, New Cracks;* Harvard University.

Made in the USA
Columbia, SC
04 September 2024

41593350R10085